BEYOND THE KNOWN

TRI THONG DANG

BEYOND THE KNOWN

The Ultimate Goal of the Martial Arts

CHARLES E. TUTTLE COMPANY
RUTLAND, VERMONT & TOKYO, JAPAN

I very much appreciate the advice of my friend and editorial consultant Dr. Jonathan Pearce in the preparation of this book.

Epigraphs for chapters eight and eleven courtesy of The Overlook Press. Chapters nine and fourteen courtesy of Kodansha International.

All illustrations are by the author.

Published by the Charles E. Tuttle Company, Inc.
of Rutland, Vermont & Tokyo, Japan
with editorial offices at
2-6 Suido 1-chome, Bunkyo-ku, Tokyo 112

LCC Card No. 92-62459
ISBN 0-8048-1891-6

First edition, 1993
Fifth printing, 1994

Printed in Japan

CONTENTS

Acknowledgments

I have been privileged to study martial art from my youth with many fine teachers, some of them internationally celebrated, others almost unknown in the larger community but equally elegant in their simplicity, integrity, and devotion to martial art. Whether my tenure of study with a teacher involved years of work or but a few seminars, each of those great masters taught me something more of the *Tao*. Among those who awakened in me the utmost feeling of discipleship were Master Morihei Ueshiba (1883–1969) and Master Chiu-Chuk Kai (1900–1991). They inspired much of what in the following work is represented in the life, work, and personality of Master Tai-Anh. It is to the spirit of universal harmony that these two masters exemplified in their lives that I dedicate this volume.

Introduction

A big toad had spent his youth at the dim bottom of a deep well, bullying the frogs and growing ever more arrogant about his size and power. One day the toad fell into the bucket and was drawn up into the light where he saw a whole new world and creatures larger and more powerful than he. Amazed and fearful, he threw himself back into the well saying, "Perhaps I'm not much after all, but these frogs will never know!"

—Vietnamese Folk Tale

IN ANCIENT times the East produced two basic inquiries concerning human life: one having to do with the life of one's spiritual being, and the other addressing the life that relates to other human beings. On the one hand, the Indians plunged into an exploration of the deepest part that lies within each individual; on the other hand, the Chinese have made the long journey seeking appropriate principles and systems for a way of living that might conciliate conflicts and rivalries among groups of people. Whatever the approach, both cultures began from a common point of interest: humankind.

Humans do not seem to be designed either to withdraw from the world or to ignore the inner voice. Humans are obligated to confront both the personal and the social. The irritations and anxieties those confrontations create have necessitated the invention of ethics and morality.

Ethics in Asian philosophy are central to both the personal life and the social life, providing standards of conduct and character, governing the judgment of good and evil, influencing choice of action, helping human beings to move harmoniously in society, in order to enable the most pleasant and useful life, personally and socially. It is along these ethical lines that the martial arts as originated in the East have offered the world their contribution to society and the individual. The Western world, however, has viewed the martial arts in a very different light.

In the West, a person seeking martial-arts instruction often goes after it like a shopper in a shopping mall. In the West one is likely to enter a school of martial arts with the same attitudes and some of the same expectations with which one enters a department store, sometimes with credit card in hand. One may bargain with the clerk, pay the money, learn the routines, take the merchandise, and leave the store. That's all there is to learning martial arts, the merchandisers appear to say.

Training in the martial arts as one finds it in this "mall" approach is often a purely mechanical process with no true human contact between the seller and the buyer, merely one more transaction in a day's busy schedule for both. In terms of the essence of martial-arts study, however, it is not that simple at all. In fact, the relationship between students and teacher in the Eastern tradition is quite complex and extraordinary because the true teacher doesn't sell knowledge and the true student cannot buy it.

Today martial training too often pays homage only to the outer aspect to attract more customers who might please themselves in the transient satisfactions and limelight of personal power. Such training usually progresses no farther than entertainment and disregards the necessary work toward inner growth.

Authentic study of martial arts involves intense study of the art of living and is dramatically different from business transactions. We know we have strayed far from the true martial arts when students and teachers, having launched the transaction as a business venture, demonstrate concern only about appearance, showing-off with spectacular combat techniques designed merely to impress others, while neglecting the cultivation of mindfulness, compassion, and love. This crass attitude makes old martial-arts masters complain that nowadays people are merely infatuated with martial arts and train to compete only in order to gain a prize or win a colored belt or title. It seems they have lost the original meaning, the serious purpose, and vitality of the martial arts. The art remains art in name only.

In a very real sense, these old masters are quite correct in their assessment, and most competent young martial-arts instructors will agree that the greatest failure in the adoption by Westerners of Eastern practice has to do with the general absence in Western teaching of ethics, values, and the art of living. Too often, the martial arts as presented in the West mean combat, self-defense, and war games involving violence-oriented, aggressive fighting. Only rarely does one find that martial-arts instruction in the Western world actually speaks to the art of living and to the inner-quest for courage and authenticity.

Today, true seekers after the martial arts are very likely to find themselves lost in darkness and frustration, left alone to identify with the appearance, the outside, but never to live in the center of their beings. Perhaps those frivolous, externally glamorous, and false ideas about the martial arts spring from commercial schools and mass media coverage, especially from movies and television which usually focus on the sensational and self-serving aspects of training while paying scant attention to the essence and intrinsic value of the training itself. How otherwise could one come to view the martial arts as aggressive, when the true teachings prize the importance of human existence, hold each individual responsible for personal actions and their consequences, and call for the ethical, moral, and spiritual advancement of all persons, regardless of race, class, gender, nationality, or religious affiliation?

When one comprehends the true nature of martial arts, one is fully aware that authentic teachings forbid devaluing, hurting, or destroying the tiniest living creature that crawls at our feet, not to speak of maiming or taking the life of another human being. It is one of the awful ironies of our age that martial-arts training that evolved over the centuries into a supremely elegant system centered on attention to ethics, morality, and right living should now be conducted in terms of techniques and gimmicks of fighting as means to destructive ends, rather than as ends in themselves.

The external and the technical tricks without the heart and the spirit amount to nothing and set the stage for forms of karma which, for the newcomer in arrogant pursuit of power, are painful and even terrifying to contemplate. It is in this light that the story of Master Tai-Anh and his student Lam is offered. The story is intended to be a karmic tale of arrogance and love, of power-lust and compassion, of teacher and student linked in a life-long karmic search for the *Tao*.

At some point in our training we reach a place where the choice is ours: to jump back, like the toad of the fable, into the dark well of our own egos where we can pretend to be master, though that place may be tiny and insignificant; or to open ourselves to the light of the infinite universe and to the teachings themselves with hearts that are open and pulsing with life.

To you who are in pursuit of the deeper teachings and of inner growth, let us set aside that figment we know as Appearance. Let us now attend to the heart of the matter, as we recognize that the growth of art flowers exclusively from within. This book will speak to all true seekers of the essence of martial-arts training, be they from West or East.

No one could describe this artistry, no words exist which could capture the magnificence of this performance.

Chapter 1

The False Path

A poor man one day met an old friend who had
become an immortal. After hearing his friend
complain of his poverty, the immortal pointed his
finger at a brick by the roadside, and the brick
immediately turned into a gold ingot. The immortal presented the gold ingot to his friend. When
the poor man was not satisfied with this, the
immortal gave him a great lion crafted of solid
gold. But the poor man was still not appeased.
"What more do you want?" asked the immortal in
frustration. "I want your finger!" was the reply.

—Shiao Fu

LAM HAD begun as servant to the eminent National
Teacher, Master Tai-Anh, who had tutored Lam on
the path of martial-arts training. Lam had practiced
hard, taken full advantage of his natural endowments,
and had himself become a very well-known martial-arts
practitioner, famous for his fabulous techniques of
encounter and combat. It was rumored in the town that
Lam must be one of the best combatants in the city,
perhaps one of the best combatants anywhere.

Lam relished the rumors of the townsfolk. Because
he had in fact excelled in his training with the sword, he

left Master Tai-Anh's tutelage, and quickly began his own school. On the strength of his reputation in the town, students rushed to his new school to sign up for classes. The school could not handle the rush of students, so Lam signed on assistant instructors and began another school, and then another, and yet another.

A wealthy resident of the town wanted his two children to be trained by Lam, for he had observed the teacher in action and was much impressed with what he saw. All the wonderful things he had heard rumored in the city were obviously true, and he enrolled his children in the school and watched their practice from the sidelines.

One day the parent was struck with an idea and, being used to implementing his ideas, he confronted Lam with the question, "Who is your instructor, Teacher Lam? The art of your master must be superior to yours, and I want the best for my children. Money is no object. Please tell me his name and how I can get in touch with him."

"Master Tai-Anh is my teacher," replied Lam, "I have not seen him in some time, and he conducts no school, no classes. He teaches only when he feels like it. He is an eccentric person, one of many moods. Getting him to teach your children is not possible."

Not one to be put off, the wealthy patron was finally successful in convincing Lam to at least accompany him to see Master Tai-Anh and ask for himself. But when the two reached Master Tai-Anh's cottage, a place at some distance, the Master refused to see them, shutting the door abruptly in their faces. Determined to try again as soon as an opportunity presented itself, Lam's patron and Lam settled down behind some shrubbery near the Master's cottage.

When the moon appeared in the starry sky, Lam and his traveling companion watched covertly as Master Tai-Anh appeared in the yard to exercise. Master Tai-Anh displayed exquisite martial artistry of a wholly unconventional form. The performance that amazed the secret watchers contained elements of all martial-arts disciplines, but it was nevertheless unique.

Fascinated, Lam's customer exclaimed, "Incredible! Truly incredible! No one could describe this artistry, no words exist which could capture the magnificence of this performance!" Lam's customer was so over-whelmed that tears gathered in his eyes. After twenty minutes of exercise, Master Tai-Anh simply returned to the cottage, shut the door, and was seen no more.

On the return to the city, the two were silent for many minutes. Then the wealthy customer said to Lam, "When I saw your work at the school, I was amazed at how splendid and spectacular your techniques were. Your directions to your students were so clear and so easy to understand, I could not imagine anything better. But now, after seeing Master Tai-Anh in action, I must conclude that you cannot in any way be compared to such a magnificent artist."

Lam smiled wryly. "It is not difficult to understand the difference between my master and me. Master Tai-

Anh performs the art only for art's sake, which is the artless art. Only that art without artfulness can give birth to real art, for real art is grounded in the spiritual, in the purposeless. It has no conditions. It is free, like air in the sky. In such moments of selfless artistic creation as we saw at the cottage yard, there is something so mysteriously exquisite that the ordinary untrained mind cannot absorb it. It cannot be told, cannot be transferred, and even the Master himself cannot express it in words alone.

"Only unimportant and superficial things can be talked about and shown to another person. The essential and profound cannot be captured in mere words. This is the reason it is beyond you, sir." Lam paused for a moment and then continued, "Perhaps it is still beyond me, too.

"I teach and perform the art for a purpose, for gain: money, fame, power, and prestige. I am beginning to understand that although my teaching of technique is easy to understand and emulate, my performance is gaudy fluff, cotton candy, a bag of tricks not to be confused with true martial art. As a martial artist I am like a boat drifting in the middle of the lake, while Master Tai-Anh has already crossed to the other shore."

Lam's confession of following a false path was sincere, yet he delighted in continuing to walk that crooked road and reap its transitory rewards. His techniques were indeed sensational, he dazzled the eyes of onlookers, and his talks stimulated the ambitions of his students. But in his heart, Lam knew that despite the material prizes he had acquired, and despite the praise and prosperity he enjoyed, his deeper self was shrunken and small. He was continuing to choose a life empty of meaning and direction.

Although he presented himself as a disciple of the renowned Master Tai-Anh, Lam was now painfully aware that Master Tai-Anh did not consider him to be a true disciple. A disciple would not have had the door slammed in his face. For Lam, the key to higher knowledge and spiritual unfolding still remained hidden in the Master's pocket, out of Lam's limited reach. That key would not be his until he was free from attachment to certain human frailties.

Such things as money, power, prestige, and fame all have their place in life, perhaps under the right circumstances, a respectworthy place. But for Lam they had become objects that blocked his movement to higher knowledge. For the present, Lam was too blinded by the trophies, the grades, and the public acclaim to be able to experience the inner world of consciousness and spirit that is born of discipline and attentiveness.

Lam still required an initiation into the soul of martial art, and this initiation could happen only in the unique relationship which develops over time between master and student during discipleship. Lam had separated himself from Master Tai-Anh and thus from the necessary discipleship.

The notion of discipleship is often rejected by

people of the Western world where independence, competitiveness, and individuality are so highly valued. In the Eastern world, however, discipleship is a crucial stage in the development of the martial-arts practitioner. It is the testing ground, so to speak, on which the disciple must resolve incredibly challenging and often painful personal crises before discovering meaning and significance in the training. Discipleship might take many months—or many years—depending on the student's commitment and maturity.

Discipleship is in itself an art form whose purpose is to help the student remove all preconceptions and presuppositions and to go beyond ego-centered, self-serving levels of existence. Discipleship involves one's learning the art of abandonment, of renunciation, of total letting go, of surrender to what truly is at the center of the art of living.

Discipleship is very much like spiritual conversion in that its successful practice is totally dependent upon the willingness of the convert, as well as on the absence of coercion by the master. If either of these requirements is not satisfied, an unhealthy relationship is created that, sooner or later, destroys itself and everything at the heart of the training.

Becoming a disciple is no simple accomplishment. It is a very complicated matter indeed, for finding a worthy master requires seriousness of purpose and, sometimes, a long and exhausting search. There is no shopping mall one can visit to find the worthy master, no department store offering easy payment; no plastic is accepted, only the hard coin of diligence. And it must be this way.

The true search is the strikingly different first stage of authentic training in the martial arts. The true search is not simply a chasing after the master with the best combat routines, strongest physical accomplishment, most books published, or biggest organization.

The chase after glittering prizes and the showy master in which so many modern youths indulge misses what for the candidate-disciple is the most important prize of all: the authentic master, revealed through mindfulness, modesty, spiritual purity, compassion, unselfishness, impartiality, and a capacity to love and be loved.

Being truly human does not in any way depend on appearance and superficial accomplishment. It is the degree of inner spiritual purity in the quality of one's life that makes for greatness. This special purity is the quality the disciple-candidate must seek in the master of true merit.

A true master continuously practices loving-kindness, compassion, and equanimity, and cultivates these virtues in every contact with disciples. A master fears no one, nor is she or he feared. Attaining such high states of consciousness is not easy and, precisely because such masters so highly value the virtues of modesty, egolessness, and loving-kindness, their grace is often unrecognized by those around them. In a world that responds to media chatter, celebrity, and self-promotion, those who seek the virtuous life are likely to escape notice, and even if recognized as good persons, their martial artistry may be completely misunderstood.

The challenge is almost as great for the student who actually finds the right master, for that student must learn to surrender the ego and accept the teachings without resistance, without negative thought. Resistance means opposition and friction. Negativity implies denial, refusal. Should the student show signs of either of these qualities, the master might choose to withhold the teachings.

While the student resists the teachings or allows negative thoughts toward the master, the necessary harmony of the master-disciple relationship cannot be created. Inner growth can take place only when the student successfully places complete faith and trust in the master. Without the open and trusting willingness to be guided, higher knowledge can never be attained. Just as the master must be worthy of the commitment and trust of the student, the student must be worthy to receive the teachings of the master.

With deep compassion and caring for his young
disciple Tai-Anh.

Chapter 2

A Meeting of Minds

A man was about to leave to take up an official post. A close friend came to see him off. "One thing you must remember when you become an official," said the friend, "is that you must always be patient."

The man replied that he certainly would. His friend then repeated his good advice three times, and three times the man nodded in assent. When for the fourth time his friend repeated the counsel, the man became angry and said, "Do you take me for an idiot? Why do you repeat such a simple thing over and over again?"

His friend sighed. "It is not easy to be patient, see?" he said. "I have said that only a few times, and here you are already impatient!"

—Shue Tao

CONCEALED IN the shrubbery and awed by Master Tai-Anh's stunning display of martial artistry, Lam began to realize that he had lost his way on the path. He could not know that while a young student-in-training, Master Tai-Anh himself had also wrestled with a similar lesson and had been led to some life-transforming insights.

A student for several years in a celebrated school of the martial arts, young Tai-Anh had become frustrated and impatient with the slowness of his progress in the training. He approached the much-respected master of the school and said in exasperation, "Exactly three years ago this month, I came to you to study, Master, and you said that if I wanted to learn the martial arts, I would need to have a profound dedication, train myself well, and not desire or wait for anything. If I accomplished this, you said, beautiful things would come my way.

"Well, Master, I understood your words very well and I have devoted myself to the training for three years now. That means one thousand and ninety-five days, to be exact. And still nothing comes to me: no money, no fame, no power, not even a real mastery of the martial arts. Nothing!" Tai-Anh thrust his arms out in supplication, as though pleading for some crumb of understanding. "I am still a nobody. No one knows of me. I remain poor. I have wasted three precious years."

"Exactly," said the old Master, nodding calmly in agreement. "You have wasted your time because you have never truly grasped the point of the training. You have not weighed my words and observed my actions mindfully through these one thousand and ninety-five days, to be exact. Your training has indeed been a sham and a waste of time in some sense, but the waste is because of your precious ego."

Tai-Anh scowled, puzzlement mixed with humiliation, as the Master pursued the lesson. "The question is not the number of days you have trained," continued the Master. "The question is how you have trained. The quest is never to capture a bunch of fighting techniques and technical terms, rather the quest must always be to open your mind and your heart to the essence, to the art of living.

"Although you said that you understood my words," said the Master. "What you still fail to grasp is that understanding by itself is empty. Such understanding is just like a flower without fragrance. The quest is not simply for understanding, the quest is for being—for *be-ing*." Tai-Anh lowered his eyes from the Master's onslaught.

The Master's voice continued to fill the training hall. He cut a circle through the air with an outstretched finger. "You chase money and fame and power like a crazed snake chasing its own tail. I warned you not to long for these things, for desire always gives birth to frustration. I urged you not to wait for these things, for waiting is bondage. Frustration and bondage are barriers to your progress. Your efforts become meaningless, Tai-Anh."

The Master turned his head and gazed out the window. The city lay below them. "All the prizes of the world are yours when you give up striving for them, Tai-Anh. But such glories will have become meaningless when at last you truly comprehend this truth, for in struggling to focus only on your art, you will have extinguished your ego. Then you will be free. That is all there is to it."

The Master paused for what seemed like forever to the impatient Tai-Anh, then concluded the lesson. "This flies in the face of logic, does it not, Tai-Anh? As well it should, because it is insight based on paradox. When you simply focus on right living and right understanding, things will come to you, whether you want them or not.

"Counting your days or weeks or months in training is as pointless as counting grains of sand. Your quest is not for quantity of production. Your quest, my quest, the martial-arts quest is for quality of experience. Follow a sincere commitment and be loyal to your most deeply felt values, and beautiful and profound experiences will be yours. Chase after those experiences, however, and they will catch you, like the snake biting its tail. Waste no more time, Tai-Anh. Be quiet, be patient, trust in your commitment, and train faithfully."

Young Tai-Anh retired slowly and respectfully from the Master's presence. He resolved that he would take to heart the Master's counsel.

The confusion of the young Tai-Anh is common among newcomers to the martial arts. Many of us fall into this combination of ignorance and impatience. We grasp only with great difficulty the proper direction of the training because we want to bypass the stepping stones pointed to by the master. We want to leap into the action, to the main event. Almost always such inclinations are based on shallow thought, illusions, and fantasies which we must unlearn before the effective training can proceed.

True, as we begin our training, the master is likely to demonstrate various performance routines and technical tricks for us, tricks he then insists we practice diligently, again and again. But at this time the master is withholding from us something more sophisticated and refined, something more subtle and mysterious. The master is withholding the key, knowing from long experience that we must first reach a point in the unfolding at which the teachings can be fully absorbed. The master knows from experience that at certain points in the progress of our training, essential teachings will be lost unless we can come to a meeting of minds, unless of our own volition we are prepared to nurture the flower within each of us.

Many students are prevented from recognizing the value of these key points and cannot understand the delicacy of the process. Their minds remain clouded by selfish fantasies and preconceptions. It is at these moments, as in comparison of our present achievement with our fantasies, that we are most likely to quit, to abandon the quest even before we comprehend that there must be a quest. To the seasoned master, however, our quitting is not a sign of failure on either part. It is simply a recognition that the time is not yet right. To those who find it necessary, quitting offers a respite from the frustration born of trying to impede the river against its natural flow.

There was another pre-eminent lesson for Tai-Anh during the early days of his training at the school, a lesson in responsibility and about being in the here-and-now.

A martial-arts tournament had been organized in a neighboring city. Young Tai-Anh and a previously unknown youth named Mai were slated to meet in the final contest. The air in the school was charged with anticipation, and the students were excited, for in the city Tai-Anh was becoming well-known as a martial artist. He felt powerful and proud.

Mai, on the other hand, was an anonymous trainee from another school who was appearing for the first time in a tournament trial. No one in the city had seen Mai in action. No one in Tai-Anh's school had even heard of Mai. Tai-Anh was puffed with self-importance. "This will be a piece of cake," he thought.

On the final day of the tournament, the day that would determine the championship, Tai-Anh was preparing for the contest with Mai. He overheard some townspeople among the onlookers gossiping that Mai had "just returned from overseas" after a year of "special and intense training" with "some of the greatest masters in the field." Behind his outward calm, Tai-Anh suddenly began to become worried and flustered.

Soon the gossip hit home. Tai-Anh's mind swirled in a flurry of questions and answers. Each question led to two or more answers, each answer led to two or more additional questions, on and on, round and round. "I wonder if it is true that Mai has just returned from special, intense training. I wonder where, with whom, China? Japan? what teacher, the one in Korea? and what kind of training? something never seen before?" Tai-Anh's thoughts spun like monkeys chattering in the trees. Tai-Anh could not stop them.

Young Tai-Anh lost the contest to Mai, along with the trophy and the title which he had so passionately desired. He felt the loss bitterly. He felt humiliated, doubtful of his art, shaken to his core.

Ashamed and angry, Tai-Anh rushed to his Master's residence, burst through the door and began to pace back and forth, demanding from the Master reasons which might explain his shameful defeat. The Master sat quietly as Tai-Anh recounted his torment.

When Tai-Anh concluded his diatribe and stood drained of emotion, the Master, instead of offering answers or explanations, quick as lightning stood up and loosed a series of powerful blows aimed at Tai-Anh's head and torso, followed by successive attacks from every direction, allowing Tai-Anh no opportunity but to try to avoid the blows and kicks by dodging and skirting left, right, up, down. The Master pressed on with more and more telling blows, finally driving Tai-Anh into a corner.

Wanting only to get out of this unexpected encounter, Tai-Anh began to fight back with all his skill. Facing the furious counterattack, the Master was soon required to give way and then to withdraw. The withdrawal was only apparent, however, for the Master redirected all his energies toward his student and totally reversed the encounter, mercifully subduing Tai-Anh with a very simple but effective series of strokes. The Master calmly walked away, leaving Tai-Anh lying breathless and disoriented on the ground.

In that instant, Tai-Anh realized that the captivating mind games he had played preceding the tournament had created an immobilizing fear, followed first by ego-deflation and embarrassment at losing the contest, and then by rage directed at the Master. But why target the Master for such anger? for not providing liability insurance against Tai-Anh's failure? As the insight formed, that Tai-Anh was not an extension of his Master but was, instead, fully and completely responsible for the consequences of his own behavior, tears flooded his eyes and he then began to weep in gratitude.

If Tai-Anh had possessed a typically Western attitude toward his training in the martial arts, this humiliating confrontation with the Master, especially following on the heels of the first humiliation at the hands of Mai, would have surely brought a quick break-up of the relationship. In the Western world, Tai-Anh might even have consulted an attorney to file a lawsuit against the Master for assault and battery, or perhaps for attempted mayhem.

For the student to seek someone to blame and sue in order to smooth his own bruised ego might be predictable from one seeking personal glory instead of *The Way*. A lawsuit against the Master would clearly demonstrate the fact that Tai-Anh had entirely missed the point of confrontation. Instead, Tai-Anh was overjoyed with this apparent mistreatment by his trusted teacher. The encounter had opened his mind and heart to new ways of being. Tai-Anh had reached an important and critical phase in his understanding of the art of simply *be-ing* in the here-and-now.

People unacquainted with authentic martial-arts training will have seen the behavior of the Master in this situation as at least bizarre. After all, a rude but sincere student had come begging for help with his problems and had received from his Master only blows and kicks. What fault had Tai-Anh to deserve such treatment? How could a master behave so ruthlessly, heartlessly, coldly?

One must pause for deeper reflection on the facts. Is it possible that the apparently heartless Master actually behaved in this instance with compassion? The Master could have simply walked away from Tai-Anh's ranting. He could have directed Tai-Anh out the door of his residence, indifferent to Tai-Anh's crisis of confidence. But the Master did neither. Instead, he acted out of his deep compassion and caring for the young Tai-Anh.

Sometimes we present to others a hard, seemingly impenetrable shell, as the Master presented himself to Tai-Anh. The Master could have enveloped Tai-Anh in softness and compassion, his real nature, but he chose to bring Tai-Anh to confront the hard-shelled product of the games created by Tai-Anh's own inflated ego. The Master knew that he would not harm Tai-Anh, for Tai-Anh had the skills necessary to protect himself in combat. The Master was after something entirely different from physical victory.

Thrown forcefully to the ground, Tai-Anh could there take advantage of the crack in his cocooned consciousness and be truly, if momentarily, awakened to the awareness that it was not lack of skill that led to his defeat by Mai. It was the maddening self-chatter of an ego-inflated mind which had immobilized him. Forced into dealing with the Master's totally unexpected action, Tai-Anh had thus to deal with the here-and-now, without thinking, without strategies, without chatter.

On numerous occasions in our lives we cannot rely on words alone. Words so often turn into grains of sand blowing loose in the wind or gathered into quicksand. Circumstances may insist that we deal in action, in the here-and-now. The Master, with great wisdom, had created for Tai-Anh just such an opportunity. The sudden attack left Tai-Anh no time to think, no time to use the logical mind, no time to be confused by self-chatter. Instead, in that moment thanks to the situation, Tai-Anh was pressed into defending against each and every blow by the Master and into fighting back vigorously with the natural mind, the embodied mind, the spiritual mind, in the awareness and wisdom which springs from the deep unconscious.

The Master's strange way of teaching invoked in Tai-Anh deep insight into his own neurotic ways. As a result of the Master's eccentric lesson, Tai-Anh began to comprehend that the essence of fighting technique demands that we avoid the seduction and attachment of personal fears and desires, that we do our best to free ourselves from such inner obstacles and snares.

Tai-Anh was sent out to confront the intruders, then returned victorious.

Chapter 3

3

BEYOND THE BOUNDS OF INTELLECT

The softest substance in the world
Goes through the hardest.
That which is formless penetrates that which
   allows no entry;
Because of this truth I know the benefit of taking
   no action.
Teaching without words
And the benefit of taking no action
Are without compare in the universe.

—Lao-tse

As THE SCHOOL to which Tai-Anh belonged flourished and became known throughout the land, a number of rival schools launched an attack against the Master's school, hoping to destroy it along with what they considered to be all of its radical teachings.

The Master called all the senior students to the training hall and shared his concern about the threats to the school. Then the Master motioned Tai-Anh to the head of the class and taught him a course in swordsmanship. The Master used the double-edged sword to perform a set of routines while Tai-Anh watched intently, concentrating on the Master's every move.

Although the Master had described the sword routine as a new creation, it revealed nothing novel. Neither powerful nor spectacular, the routine was rather slow and soft, evocative of clouds swirling in the sky. At the end of the set, the Master turned to Tai-Anh and asked, "Did you see it?"

"Yes, Master," Tai-Anh replied.

"Do you remember everything?"

"I remember almost half of it," Tai-Anh answered.

"That's all right," replied the Master in an indifferent tone of voice. "Think about the rest!" A little while later, the Master asked Tai-Anh the same question again, "Do you remember now?"

"I have forgotten more than half of it now," Tai-Anh replied, half-embarrassed.

One of the other students who was on the scene raised the question, "Master, how could Tai-Anh remember all of a series of techniques when it was seen only once?"

The Master said not a word but instead removed his sword from its sheath and gave a second performance. This time the students stared at one another in confusion. Seeing an incomprehensible situation unfold before them, one of the disciples said, "Master, the set you have just performed was completely different from the first one. How could Tai-Anh remember all of this?"

Ignoring the question, the Master returned to Tai-

Anh. "Well, how about it? Do you remember everything?"

Embarrassed, Tai-Anh replied, "I vaguely remember only a few techniques, Master."

The Master returned to a seat while Tai-Anh walked back and forth across the floor with a thoughtful expression. Then, sudden as a flash of lightning, smiling from ear to ear, Tai-Anh straightened and, with words which seemed to speak from the innermost soul said, "I have forgotten everything, Master. Everything!"

A smile flickered across the Master's lips. Passing the most beautiful of swords to Tai-Anh, the Master ordered him to go out alone to confront and scatter the enemies. And then the Master simply walked away without saying another word.

Later, after life-and-death struggles against single and massed intruders, Tai-Anh returned victorious, bringing great glory to the school.

All the students were amazed and delighted to have witnessed Tai-Anh's astonishing success in battle, news of which had traveled far and wide. But the Master remained indifferent throughout the victory celebration. Finally, a disciple said, "Master, it seems you are not pleased that we have won the battle, thanks to Tai-Anh."

"Don't be so excited," the Master replied solemnly. "Don't be so excited."

Here we are again, with odd and seemingly senseless words by the Master. When Tai-Anh remembered the martial routine that the Master had taught him, the Master appeared disappointed. When Tai-Anh admitted forgetting everything he had been taught, the Master seemed pleased.

Later, after a glorious and successful battle from which Tai-Anh emerged the undisputed victor who brought great honor to the school, the Master revealed not a single sign of satisfaction, but muttered only, "Don't be so excited."

Is the Master simply in a bad mood? Is he distracted by illness? Or is there some deeper message accompanying these unpredictable actions? Let us review and analyze his behavior.

What the Master aimed to teach Tai-Anh was not conventional technique and routine performance, for he knew the truth of the ancient wisdom that "among the strongest there is always a stronger." Relying on the physical body trained to perform all kinds of spectacular acrobatics is obviously very important in improving the physical dimension of the martial arts. The passage of the sword through the air with whistling speed was what everyone expected when the Master demonstrated the sword routine. But what the disciples saw was slow, unimpressive.

The Master was demonstrating that our expertise with routines and tricks may deceive us into thinking those the real stuff of the martial arts. The Master no longer cared to impart this kind of surface knowledge. Instead, he concentrated on a far more important phase of the training from which Tai-Anh might penetrate into deeper realms where the art ceases to be art, where effort ends, where the reality of the here-and-now unfolds quietly, unimpeded by applause or by any sort of expectation.

At first, the Master's words and actions appeared strange and unintelligible to the students. But this experience of unintelligibility was precisely what the Master had intended to create in his disciples.

The Master demonstrated sword routines, but only when Tai-Anh admitted to remembering none of them did the Master send him to fight. The sending of a possible incompetent to defend the honor of the school caused the heads of the students to swirl with doubt and fear. However, when Tai-Anh returned to the school as the unquestioned victor, all doubting of the Master ceased.

Tai-Anh's triumph was a just reward culminating his long years of effort and struggle, but the triumph obviously did not depend on Tai-Anh's reproduction of the Master's desultory sword routines. After all, Tai-Anh admitted remembering none of them. Tai-Anh's triumph was something more than a physical or moral triumph. It was also a spiritual triumph. Only with Tai-Anh's victory did the students realize that the higher realms of the art of living embody not the sword alone, but the physical and the spiritual as one and the same.

Had Tai-Anh tried consciously to recall all he had learned, his defeat would have been the speedy result. Tai-Anh would have been able to display only techniques powered by the analytical mind, techniques that would all be compelled by conventional attitudes and limited by ordinary perception and logic.

If Tai-Anh had clung tightly to conventional techniques, this very clinging would have impeded victory by blocking the natural and fluid unfolding of Tai-Anh's movements. The result would have been failure and perhaps death.

But when Tai-Anh had reached that state in which technique is not considered, only then could he emanate from the center of his being, that place where body and mind and spirit dance as one. Only when intellect was no longer conscious, when body was no longer monitored, when spirit was no longer engaged, only then was Tai-Anh in true *mind-ful-ness* embodying the artless art and unfolding from his *one-ness*, splendidly awake.

Logic has no part whatsoever in this process. The fundamental reality, the *Tao*, always manifests itself beyond the boundaries of logic. Those who have been fully initiated can begin to understand this noble truth, that only by breaking our attachment to the mediocre can we absorb the simple truth of right living and reach for a higher realm of being.

We need to bear in mind that the techniques which we acquire as students during periods of training are only basic information which we receive on loan from the teacher. They are borrowed techniques, not our own. By themselves, borrowed techniques are the stuff of ignorance, for in employing them we only simulate the ways of others. This "monkey see, monkey do" process is required at the beginning stage of our training. But borrowing from others is acceptable only to a certain point. After we have attained a level of proficiency, we must eschew imitation. If the means are only imitations, then the ends are merely replicas. Nothing has bloomed fresh from our hearts.

Our work must always be to learn to go *beyond the known*, beyond what is borrowed, beyond our fear of pain, and beyond our desire for pats on the back to the higher knowledge, the spiritual knowledge that is intuitive, inexplicable, and beyond intellect. When we reach such moments something will happen.

Only this something beyond thinking can free us from our games and roles, our old conditioned responses, and uplift us from the well of ego into the bright illumination. This something can gain form only when the grabbing, clutching, frightened ego is subdued. The subduing of ego does not result from reasoning or logic. It comes from beyond the world of our immediate sensations and thoughts to what philosophers have called the state of immanence, the state in which reliance on the accumulation of information and technique produces only withered flowers on a tangled vine.

Only when our capacity for immanence, for compassionate intuition, is fully developed does our mountain air become filled with delicious and exotic fragrance.

In the moment when Tai-Anh entered battle on the mountainside, his mind and ego no longer existed.

With no ego to fuel the mind games, Tai-Anh's mind became empty and cherished nothing. When he began to move, an intricate ballet began to flow spontaneously, a dance filled with techniques and acrobatics never seen before.

In this state, Tai-Anh was at one with the source of all creation, blossoming out to handle in the moment each situation as it arose. His body-mind-spirit moving in perfect natural harmony reached its peak experience, its ultimate unfolding. The mind is empty and clear in such moments, and out of the emptiness emerge wonders.

Something has happened. It is the state of *no-mind* described by practitioners of the Zen tradition. It is the state of being that every martial artist prizes. The paradox here is that as we experience that state of *no-mind*, we forget it without noticing our doing so, for we are now in tune with the *Tao*, and are no longer separate egos. We merge with the *Tao* and become one with the wholeness of existence.

"Don't be so excited," is what the Master muttered upon Tai-Anh's return as the glorious victor. But what was the Master trying to tell us? Was it that Tai-Anh's victory was simply victory in one battle in which many had been wounded and killed?

Tai-Anh had indeed won a great victory, but the Master knew Tai-Anh had not won the war, and so battle after battle would continue to be fought, and more would be wounded or killed. When would such battles end? This was the Master's chief concern. How could anyone display joy while battles between and among the schools continued to rage? The tragedy would persist unless the leaders of all schools were able to abandon their arrogance, prejudice, and selfish concerns and come together as a community to work for the common good.

But the craving for wins in battle, and the desire for renown and riches, no matter how short-lived the craving, had dimmed the school leaders' intellect and confused their ability to reason. As a result, the more power they gathered, the more they craved. Having lost contact with the inner flower of spirituality and virtue, they were left with only flowery words, as though words could substitute for the spiritual presence they may once have known.

Harmony, love, and peace cannot be created out of prejudice, arrogance, and selfishness. Universal love cannot be attained by discriminating on the basis of such things as clan membership, race, gender, or philosophy. Peace needs to go hand-in-hand with goodwill. No one can realize peace who is ruled by jealously, hatred, or the desire to exploit others, most especially when that exploitation is motivated by the desire for profit.

Only by living in harmony with the *Tao*, constantly practicing calm and alert awareness, can that vital something happen. And one day in a very special moment, the seed in the ground of our being begins to germinate and penetrates the surface of our consciousness and we experience the light of the sun and the free flowing of energy through body-mind-spirit. We become free, and in this state experience new wonders. We must remember, however, that if we long for this freedom, it does not come. Only in the absence of desires and cravings may such fulfillment be realized. This is the mystery of the martial arts.

At a certain level, the best explanation is not to explain at all, and the highest communication is silence.

Chapter 4

A Union of Hearts

As we trim the light,
The dolls presenting shadows,
Each reveals its own.

—Shiki

ONE MORNING the students gathered in the training hall, waiting for the lesson of the day. The Master appeared, but during the entire hour did not say a single word and did not perform even one technique. Instead, he simply lifted a lotus flower in front of the students and remained completely silent.

As the minutes ticked away, the students became bored and bewildered, except for Tai-Anh, who alone was delighted with the Master's actions and greeted them with a gentle and discreet smile. The Master smiled in return, and that simple sharing of smiles was proof that the essential insight had been received.

In the martial arts, the relationship of Master and disciple is a peculiar one. At the beginning, we may find the training not alluring and exciting, but boring. We would be wise to remember that the beginning is but the foundation of what can become a great edifice.

As if building a house, the teacher must first pour a base of concrete to lay the foundation. Students

49

typically want to live in the house right away. Too often we have little patience to wait for the foundation even to dry so that the teacher might be able to erect the walls and attach the roof. We are in a hurry. "I want it all, and I want it now!" we say.

In order to be of value to most Westerners, space must be filled with objects. Empty space is useless and wasted unless it is to be occupied with things or with action of some kind. In the East, however, space and emptiness may be prized and trusted. Walls and floors, windows and doors comprise a house, but it is the space between them which is livable.

So, too, it is the empty spaces in Eastern works of art which are the creative centers around which things and actions take on meaning. As students, however, we are often more concerned with filling in the emptiness and putting things together.

Our hurrying is merely a sign of our immaturity, for maturity grows from our cultivating patience and perseverance, and the understanding that sometimes one must walk the path very slowly, like garden snails in the morning dew. Bringing awareness to the empty spaces in our search for meaning takes time.

As a result of their impatience, many students leave the training regimen. Those of us who remain may show glimmers of the necessary self-discipline, but we, too, are likely to grow restless for novelty. Sometimes new things do not come quickly enough. The whole structure does not appear to be exciting enough, most likely because the foundation is not yet dry, or because a change in the weather has caused a delay in the work, so the teacher, too, must exercise patience. But in time the waiting is over and the erecting of the walls and the roof begins. Slowly, we can see a shelter rising before us, sparse and bare to be sure, but shelter nonetheless. The next steps involve constructing the partitions and installing the doors, the ceilings, and so on.

Even when the structure appears to be complete, it may not be habitable—unless the plumbing, the wiring, and so forth, are accomplished so as to comply with the teacher's building codes. Every stage of the building project depends on the success of previous accomplishments. Each phase takes time. After fulfilling the requirements, even as we anticipate entering our bright new martial-arts home, we may yet encounter another crisis created by, for example, the teacher who gives ambiguous or apparently nonsensical instructions.

Instructional discourse is often abstract. It may appear too eccentric for us to grasp with our physical senses. Something in it always remains hidden from us, out of sight like the plumbing and the wiring of the house. Day after day, apparent nonsense may accompany the teacher's demonstrations. Only the teacher is aware of the hidden requirements, necessary elements which the students cannot see. The effective teacher is one who provides memorable ambiguity so that the effective student may one day make the appropriate connections.

We remain in disbelief of much that surrounds us,

until that special moment when we step on the threshold before the door which opens by some unseen force and closes behind us. A fingertip touch on the switch and the house is illuminated with radiance. Slight pressure on another control point and a cool breeze infuses the house. All these hidden devices are powered by a reality which now becomes clear to each of us who has learned to understand the mechanism or process. The teachings, which only moments ago seemed boring and nonsensical, suddenly become meaningful. We begin to believe and trust in our Master and we prepare to inhabit the new house with the Master who holds the key.

When our belief and trust reach a mature state, our third eye suddenly opens, looking inward toward what has always been beyond us. Then we are able to sense that the Master's earlier nonsense was in reality the very essence of the teachings.

From this point of enlightened consciousness forward, honest and profound communication between Master and student is not only possible, but is the only form of relationship conducive to communicating the key to higher knowledge. If there is true communication between Master and student, and a close relationship which endures and matures to an advanced stage, harmony and love will be manifest and a oneness will emerge from that seamless horizon. On the other hand, if the hearts of both Master and student are not attuned, not beating to the same rhythm, the communication cannot occur.

At times, the Master imparts the teachings slowly. As in the case of the aged Master holding the lotus flower before the class, the teacher may become silent, testing our understanding that techniques of combat are no longer needed and words are no longer necessary. Words and techniques are, after all, only vehicles to carry the message; they are not the message itself. Sometimes a simple smile, a single look, or a particular gesture are all that is needed to express the essential thoughts. At a certain level, the best explanation is not to explain at all, and the highest communication is silence.

More important than words and concepts is the union of the hearts, for the mind is often misled by the heart. The old saying is true that "the heart has its reasons which reason cannot know."

It all sounds illogical and absurd. Yet the paradoxes and absurdities mask profound realities that become intelligible only in the light of one's spiritual life. The highest knowledge is not akin to the intellectual mind and to logical reasoning. The highest knowledge comes from the heart.

Those of us who aspire to be true seekers on the path to higher knowledge must take our time to search for an authentic master. We must learn to have an open mind, to be receptive, and to learn the art of surrender which is to remove all preconceptions and to go beyond our ego-centered level of existence. Otherwise, it is better not to start on the path at all, for such a path will be crooked and will lead us astray.

The true path is a path of no return. Once we begin on the true path we must follow it to the end. The mind that creates heaven is the same mind that creates hell. We ourselves are the only source of all misunderstanding and confusion. We ourselves embody the location of all our insight and higher knowledge. Teachers and masters, whatever their teaching methods and however deep their understanding and insight, are but guides and helpers along the way.

Nothingness means not concealing preconceived
ideas and accepting the unity of good and evil, right
and wrong, like and dislike.

Chapter 5

THE VITALITY OF THE INEXPRESSIBLE

The musical tones are only five, but their melodies are too numerous to count. The basic colors are only five, but their combinations are limitless. The flavors are only five, but their blending is of such variety as to be endless. In battle the forces are only two, the regular and the special, but their combinations are infinite, and no one can comprehend them all.

—Sun Tzu

DURING A t'ai-chi praying mantis kung-fu workout, the Master, observing that Tai-Anh had reached another level in his training, explained the salient points of *zhai-yao*, a senior course of *t'ai mantis*. He described the three perspectives from which one may attempt to grasp the essence of the art: to see, to observe, and to revere. The Master said, "To see is a matter of the eye, to observe is a matter of the mind, and to revere is a matter of the soul. These perspectives are in ascending order. Those who have reached the third stage where the spiritual abides are in the essence of the art."

Eyes wide open, Tai-Anh absorbed not only the

Master's words, but also the Master's intonation, expression, gesture. "To see or to observe one must rely on the senses and must interpret the external world through acts of the intellect: choosing, summarizing, deciding. To be able to look upon the art with reverence, however, one must experiment with meditation and contemplation, allowing one's intuition to awaken and blossom. Insight is beyond psychological phenomena. It is not logical, not rational, not even mental. It is of the soul.

"When one is able even partially to identify one's being with the art, to that extent one sets aside individuality, feels communion with the art, and touches the ground of reality. To the martial artist, this perspective of reverence for the art can be taken as a sign of maturity." The Master smiled. "At that intuition, the incubation period is over, and the chicken knows the right time has arrived to peck at the egg shell. Out of that shell there comes a new generation."

The Master continued. "Why do you suppose the Buddhist monks of the famous Shao-lin Temple became so expert in martial arts? It was because their religion requires many hours a day of sitting in meditation, a focusing of attention that leads to the contemplative state."

Unsure of the Master's point, Tai-Anh asked, "Master, why contemplation? Haven't I heard you say that emptiness or nothingness is the state through which one reaches the highest level of knowledge?"

The Master replied, "I say again, contemplation is

the act of looking-upon-with-reverence without the intervention of any representative ideas. Contemplation must be independent of any reasoning processes. When this is grasped, a state of tranquillity and purity of the mind appears, allowing the emergence of true energy. And that energy is nothing else but emptiness which truly is the source of all possibilities.

"To experience this phenomenon, one must first do away with attachments, prejudices, partiality, selfishness, and avarice. Most important, one must give up the destructive notion that body, mind, and spirit are separate. Intuition can work at its best only when contemplation has discovered the emptiness from which intuition comes.

"But the whole of the learning here must be guided by a master, however confusing and mystifying his words or actions may seem. Otherwise, experiencing the intuitive state is impossible." After a short pause the Master looked closely at Tai-Anh and asked, "Do you have any questions thus far?"

"Yes, Master," Tai-Anh replied. "I think I now have a vague idea of emptiness, but not of nothingness. I beg you to explain."

"Ah!" said the Master, evidently pleased with Tai-Anh's question. "You have touched upon the quintessential part of the *Tao*, its metaphysical aspect. This is the crucial part that is always unclear to the uninitiated. Ordinary people are always so one-sided. They consider nothingness and think of a state of nothing, non-being, or non-existence. This view is superficial. Note well that nothingness possesses a transcendental component which helps one thoroughly to understand its significance. In nothingness there is the root of something, a being or an existence.

"It is the same with inactivity. Inactivity does not mean simply a state of non-activity or inertia. By its nature, the word inactivity connotes a tacit action, a latent restless motion. It has always been thus. It is the universal law of equilibrium which contains the imperceptible cosmic forces of the principle of negative and positive, yin and yang. Yin and yang are regarded as opposites, yet complementary; one cannot exist without the other. Indivisible, they constitute oneness: one but two, two but one.

"To understand this experience one must create a driving force with which to accomplish the understanding. One must employ this force to unwinnow good and evil, right and wrong, like and dislike, and so forth. Only then may one become peaceful, placid, tranquil. Living in such consciousness one becomes emancipated and is able to create all kinds of things and know perfectly well how to cope with every challenge encountered in life.

"Nothingness means not concealing preconceived ideas and accepting the unity of good and evil, right and wrong, like and dislike. When faced with duality, one remains choiceless.

"There is no such thing as liking the good and disliking the evil, or liking the right and disliking the wrong. From a practical point of view, there is no good thing that does not include roots of an evil thing. Conversely, there is no bad thing that does not have the roots of a good thing. In the same way, there is no advantage without disadvantage and no disadvantage without advantage. It is only when one comes to perceive that a positive yang is not just yang but implies a negative yin, and a negative yin is not just yin but implies a positive yang, that one can thoroughly understand the mysterious meaning of the yin-yang principle. Only when one is beyond duality will a mysterious law free one from bondage. The whole secrecy of martial art, Tai-Anh, lies in this point.

"In fact, it is not difficult to understand these things at all if one considers them intuitively." The Master sighed and smiled. "Explaining with words is almost hopeless, but one uses words and language because human beings can hardly live without them. And so whenever tackling a delicate thought associated with the spirit or the soul, a teacher must use words if only to eventually lead people to silence. Only silence can truly communicate, Tai-Anh. I am, of course, speaking monistically. The silence of which I speak is communication heart to heart. Ultimately no talk is necessary; only feeling is expressible."

"Is it true Master, that most wise persons are usually not inclined to talk a great deal and sometimes even keep complete silence?" Tai-Anh asked.

"Exactly! But take care not to confuse that silence with absence of thought. I am speaking of dynamic and eloquent silence, more eloquent than eloquence itself."

Tai-Anh appeared pensive while listening to this cryptic answer.

The Master then left the hall for his quarters, beckoning Tai-Anh to follow and continuing the lesson. "If a wise person must explain something, he usually explains briefly. But behind that brief talk may be profoundly penetrating thought. To the wise person, it is unnecessary that thoughts be expressed at length, for it is the indescribable and inexpressible thoughts which are always much more worthwhile and truthful. And—do not forget this, Tai-Anh—the thought which can be expressed is usually not the essential one. It is the inexpressible thought that is fundamentally vital. For these reasons wise people do not speak a great deal. When wise people speak, it is only to try to lead people to what cannot be said. Not only do the wise speak little, but even their brief remarks often contain cryptic and equivocal statements, statements often imbued with a special attractiveness which stimulate the hearers to wonder at the hidden meaning of those statements."

After a period of silence, the Master continued. "You have noticed that most wise people are disinclined to chatter and do not spout platitudes. This is appropriate because the wisest people tend never to rationalize a misunderstanding or give proof or apologize or defend their exposition. Their covert and overt motives are the same: simply to present opportunities for listeners to use their own potential to experiment, and so that listeners may discover their capacity to listen to the echoes that resonate deep from the center of their beings. What concerns wise people is the depth of the subject matter. Wise people are more interested in the inner voice, in intuitiveness.

"The explanations of wise people are impartial, neutral. Even though the sun indifferently and without preference casts its rays over the world to help all flowers to bloom, yet each plant has its own unique flower and fragrance. In the same way, each individual human being has a unique way of awakening, growing."

"But, Master, after all what does emptiness have to do with martial-arts training?" Tai-Anh asked.

"When no thought of unhappiness or happiness, like or dislike is stirred in the mind, emancipation follows, and one is able to create all kinds of things, including martial art. Every Eastern art, whether it be literary, pictorial, musical, or martial, has its own mystery because all have been greatly influenced by the concepts of nothingness and emptiness. Because of this, artists have tended to illustrate the infinite things in the universe in simple ways. Perhaps there may be a more productive way of explaining this. Let me consider for a moment," said the Master.

A single sound would be sufficient to confuse my
opponent's mind and turn upside down all the vessels
and meridians in his body.

Chapter 6

THE IRRELEVANCE OF THE INSTRUMENT OF COMBAT

"Hui Zhi is forever using parables," complained someone to the Prince of Liang. "If you, Sire, forbid him to speak in parables, he won't be always so irritatingly indirect." The prince agreed with this critic. The next day the prince saw Hui Zhi. "From now on," said the prince, "kindly talk in a straightforward manner, and not in parables."

"Suppose there were a man who did not know what a catapult is," replied Hui Zhi. "If he asked you what it looked like, and you told him it looked just like a catapult, would he understand what you meant?" "Of course not," answered the prince.

"But suppose you told him that a catapult looks something like a bow and that it is made of bamboo—wouldn't he understand you better?"

"Yes, that would be clearer," admitted the prince.

"We compare something a man does not know with something he does know in order to help him to understand it," said Hui Zhi. "The truth is always just beyond our grasp anyway, but if you won't let me use parables, how can I even try to make things clearer to you?" The prince agreed that Hui Zhi was right.

—Liu Shiang

THE MASTER looked about the room, smiled, and nodded to himself. "Tai-Anh," he said, "look at the painting on the wall over there and tell me what you see."

Tai-Anh moved toward the wall, observed the painting for long moments, and said, "It represents a wise man standing on a cliff contemplating nature and, at the foot of the cliff, some sort of fighting is in progress." Tai-Anh took a few steps back and continued. "Master, I can see something else. This piece of art was painted with a remarkable vital force. Through these few marvelous strokes, the painting has revealed the artist's temperament and depicted the mysterious work of the sword."

Tai-Anh gazed steadily at the painting for a while longer and at last remarked, "Those strokes are so lively. They are so energetic but also vacillating, aggressive but courteous, audacious but bashful. The artist had probably fallen into the realm of emptiness while creating this masterpiece." Tai-Anh was almost as pleased with his observation as with the painting and finished his comment whispering, "A divine brush. Quite a divine brush!"

Sitting in an armchair, the Master quietly jiggled his knees in approval and said. "Yes, Tai-Anh, divine indeed. Yes. This piece of art was painted by a celebrated swordsman. He once told me he painted this when he became intoxicated by a flow of some sort of verve during martial-art training. Without intention, his swordsmanship became manifest in his brush. He said that this masterpiece is unique in his artistic life. After he recovered from his hangover, he tried and tried to paint again but was unable to produce a similar work."

Tai-Anh interrupted, asking, "A real work of art like this, why didn't the artist sign his name, Master?"

"As he was not present at the painting, Tai-Anh, he could hardly sign his name," replied the Master patiently. "For the most stupendous deeds of a human being can be produced only when he or she falls into emptiness and thereby forgets the self." "Oh," said Tai-Anh. Tai-Anh was unclear as to the meaning of the Master's answer. But suddenly he recalled the time in which a number of attackers had threatened his school. The Master had sent young Tai-Anh alone, seemingly against all odds, to defend the school. Tai-Anh had returned as the undisputed winner, vanquishing all challengers. Although an obvious victor, Tai-Anh could not totally recall his experience or fully understand the entire meaning of his victory. Was his astonishing achievement due to his technical skill or had something original and creative grown out of his own consciousness during combat? Could it be that Tai-Anh's situation was like this painter's empty-mindedness? Tai-Anh pondered this problem.

Although technique is often understood to be the means leading to an end, in his epic combat Tai-Anh had become transfigured, and the very meaning of technique as it is commonly used became irrelevant. Because he had lost his self, his individuality, his technique, he had won the battle. Now, looking at the painting, Tai-Anh easily recognized therein the artistic spirit of swordsmanship, and his demonstrated maturing of comprehension pleased the Master very much.

"Not bad. Not bad at all!" the Master muttered. Delighted at this comment, Tai-Anh found the courage to ask, "Master, how did this painting come into your possession?"

"The artist presented it to me as a memento," replied the Master. "As I have said, the artist was not only a famous painter, but was also well-versed in the musical arts. He was also known to be very competent in swordsmanship. One day he was confronted by a young swordsman with a challenge: if the artist could best this challenger with the sword, he would earn a precious piece of music.

"The young challenger said that the piece of music had been written by the famous composer An Thy shortly after he had suffered a long fit of fever. The challenger said, 'During the time of his illness, An Thy realized that the common idea of loving life and fearing death was no longer a matter of concern with him. An Thy then abandoned everything, including even his self-consciousness. Upon his doing so, a musical fever suddenly overcame him, and he composed the piece with extraordinary speed. It is a refined, exquisite instrumental work, very rare in the world.'

"Bedazzled by the offer, the painter said, 'Is that true? A work of An Thy? You must know then that I am fond of music.' The challenger handed the music score to the painter who examined it respectfully, page by page.

"'So, this composition is indeed that of An Thy,' the painter said. 'Having been in seclusion for years, I did not realize such a masterpiece existed.' He suddenly stopped turning the pages. 'How can this segment be written to be played at such a tempo? Surely no one can play these notes at the designated speed!'

"The challenger explained that, although the composition was fairly new, it had been played many times in public and its performers remarked that the music almost plays itself despite its technically difficult appearance on the page. Almost unconsciously, the painter repeated, 'Are you really offering me this music?'

The challenger responded, 'That is correct, given the condition that you best me in combat!'

"The painter was puzzled. 'I want to ask you one more question,' he said. 'Who suggested me to you?'

"'Only minutes before he died,' responded the challenger, 'the composer of this masterpiece entrusted it to my temporary care and advised me to search for a deserving person to become its owner. Allow any who wish to perform it to do so, he said, but find a deserving person to become its owner. He did not specify a particular person. You are a respected gentleman and well-versed in music. I am happy that this music might find a truly worthy keeper. Shall we begin?'"

The Master continued his tale. "The painter told me that although it was a closely-matched and hard-fought combat, in the end he prevailed and received the musical score. Years later, as he roamed this area and heard in the garden the resonant sound of my lute, he entered and greeted me as a musical companion, saying that he had something wonderful to share with me. However, when he caught a glimpse of the sword I was wearing on my back, he appeared especially delighted and asked for a friendly duel before showing me the music. I agreed.

"The painter said, 'Let's try a few techniques, with no intent to hurt each other, of course.' He used his flute as his weapon, and I my lute. He swung the flute into the air making a soft sound which began to lull me to sleep. I plucked on my lute to disperse the soothing sound and lashed out, aiming at his shoulder. He dodged the attack, using the flute to hit the mortal point *chi-ch'uan* under my armpit. If the flute had truly hit the target I would have suffered a severe pain in my heart, but the painter withdrew the flute just in time, and attacked the *shaohai* point under my elbow in an attempt to numb my arm. I successfully avoided the thrust.

"Because the painter was afraid his flute might suffer damage, he withdrew, and I also withdrew to avoid a collision with the flute. Both of us, however, had proved to be respectful adversaries. Then I changed tactics by attacking the *binao* point of his left elbow. He riposted by thrusting at the *tiantu* point in my neck, but I raised my instrument, fending off the blow. He immediately withdrew the flute in time. The fight went on and on and became quite exciting.

"I then twanged on the lute in a pressed tune. In performing that tune I used a supreme internal power in an attempt to confuse my opponent's mind. By my applying this type of melody, my opponent's strength of mind would diminish; if my play arose softly, my opponent would move slowly. Strangely enough, he used techniques completely contrary to the sounds of my lute. The more he speeded up his techniques, the more I softened and relaxed the sound of my lute. This harmonious countering caused my opponent to fall into a defenseless situation.

"By means of diligent practice over several years, my synchronizing the sound of the lute with the movements of martial art had already reached a high level. If it could reach its ultimate peak, however, it would be unnecessary to fight, for at that point a single sound from the lute would be sufficient to confuse my opponent's mind, turn upside down all the vessels and meridians in his body, produce a state of vertigo and, eventually, coma. I perceived that my opponent was feeling the power of my art. He became terrified and dizzy and suddenly fearful that I would hurt him."

The Master continued his story. "I plucked my lute

loudly, producing a strange resonance that came close to frightening the painter out of his wits. At that very moment he shouted sharply, then sank at once to the kneeling position wearing a haggard expression. I arose silently, holding my lute and regarding it with surprise, for I saw that the painter's shout had broken all the strings of my lute, while the lute's destructive sound had caused the agitation of the painter's circulatory system. Neither of us said a word about the outcome of our combat. In silence each of us appreciated the other's skills.

"After that encounter, we became good friends and played music together for months. Before his departure, he formally presented this painting to me."

There is no need to struggle to be free, the absence of struggle is in itself freedom.

Chapter 7

A Transformation

A schoolboy was playing truant in the street
when he saw an old woman grinding an iron
pestle on a stone. Being curious, the boy asked
the old woman what she was doing. "I am going
to grind this pestle into a needle to sew cloth
with," answered the old woman. The child
laughed. "But this is such a big pestle, how can
you hope to grind it down to a needle?" "It
doesn't matter," replied the old woman. "Today I
grind it, tomorrow I'll grind it again, and the day
after tomorrow again. The pestle will get smaller
every day, and one day it will be a needle." The
child saw the point and went to school.

—Ch'en Len-shi

FOLLOWING YEARS of training with the Master, Tai-
Anh returned to his hometown where he began to teach
the martial arts. Forsaking his other talents and
opportunities, Tai-Anh chose the martial-arts path as a
meaningful way to fulfill his destiny. One may imagine
how happy he was as adoring young students flocked to
his classes, seeking his guidance and teaching.

Time passed slowly for Tai-Anh. One morning,
during meditation, he pondered the values and the

75

meaning found in the work of teaching. He began to feel concern that the teachings he imparted to his many students were tedious and shallow. Enmeshed in the daily routines of earning a living, pressed by meetings and membership in various organizations, confronted with ever more rules and regulations to follow, Tai-Anh began to experience an emptiness in his heart.

Tai-Anh felt that he was losing something—freedom, freewill, meaning, spaciousness in life. Something was missing. All Tai-Anh seemed to do, day in and day out, was to impart knowledge to others and to watch the ticking clock as he ran the daily treadmill of meetings, classes, memos, and so on. But there was no new knowledge brought to him. He was creating nothing special. Nothing fresh or juicy was emerging from his work. Certainly his developing and teaching many sophisticated and spectacular routines of fighting techniques brought him some immediate fulfillment, but this very gratification was growing into an impassable obstacle to his advancing to newer and deeper levels of knowledge.

Tai-Anh's mind spun with endless self-questioning, with hungry feeling and repetitious thoughts about his shortcomings, deficiencies, and imperfections. He felt that something subtle but vital was slipping away, and he became first melancholy and then deeply depressed and confused. This state of mind, the knotted feelings of being defective and inadequate, persisted for years until Tai-Anh willed himself to break through the mirrored windows that hid the great beyond.

Tai-Anh began to understand the love of learning and teaching in a new way, a fresh way. What Tai-Anh had believed to be love of learning was not love in its truest sense, but rather the driving force of desire for selfish gain, personal satisfaction, power, prestige, and an unquenchable hunger to be the big toad, however small the well.

Tai-Anh's many hours of newly-disciplined meditation and contemplation had begun to clear his overstuffed mind, making room for the serendipitous but profound insight that his love was conditional, not a true and infinite love, but a reflection of the ego's ambitions and strategies. Tai-Anh came to see clearly that as soon as these conditions were brought to the fore, the love diminished and finally disappeared into a bottomless abyss. In these quiet moments of meditation Tai-Anh acknowledged that greedy, grasping impulses must be banished if a loving path to the beyond were to be traveled at all.

Regardless of his martial prowess, Tai-Anh had been a frightened man for many years. Doubt and self-argument had raged within him. But in the midst of his confusion and anguish, a calm voice inside him kept urging him to continue his search. Tai-Anh simply sat quietly in meditation, watching his breath rise and fall as thoughts, feelings, and sensations rose and burst like bubbles on a lake.

Tai-Anh quieted his perplexity and confusion one day at a time. Fear, insecurity, and even occasional disaster ceased to alarm him. He dismissed, abolished each illusion passing through his mind. He remembered the dictum, "There is no need to struggle to be free. The absence of struggle is in itself freedom." Loyal to this chosen path, Tai-Anh found himself well-off, comfortable, and at ease.

Then, during a workout one evening, Tai-Anh experienced the coursing of strange new feelings and sensations enabling every technique he performed to be so precise, so perfect, so fluid, so totally beyond what he had imagined possible, as to seem miraculous. This stunningly superior accomplishment persisted until the day he was asked to explain how his performance had become suddenly so astonishingly more effective, precise, and graceful. He attempted to explain, and from that moment he was no longer able to perform with his previous brilliance.

Tai-Anh pondered on all the feelings he experienced during his first miraculous workout. Though Tai-Anh was in complete ignorance of the cause of his wonderful, if temporary, special facility, he believed he had reached a peak that evening. He was puzzled at his loss, but with his mature ability to reflect without words he was not devastated.

Some months later the same wonderful sensations returned. And again Tai-Anh was unsuccessful in his efforts to define those sensations, to guard them, to hoard them. Finally, after attempt upon vain attempt to recapture those moments of grace, he was left with only his everyday cluttered and greedy mind. Or so it seemed to him.

Though unable to interpret his brief epiphanies accurately, Tai-Anh gradually began to see the world differently. He came to realize that the moment one's mind entered a state of absolute freedom from external or internal pressure, once one no longer clung to the conventional, to power games, once one no longer hungered for anything whatsoever, only then could one experience mindful synchronicity with the ordinary activities of daily life. Tai-Anh had found a crack in his wall of pain.

Very slowly Tai-Anh began to experience the exquisite internal stillness which enables the experience of being thoroughly aware of one's embodiment from moment to moment, of being able to sense precisely the body's movements, feelings, and thoughts which give form and meaning to each and every living moment.

For years Tai-Anh lived the outwardly conventional life, keeping secret these mysterious interior happenings out of concern that ignorant people would demean him and cause the loss of his livelihood. Once or twice he sought counsel from friend or family member, but he discovered that others were no help, that they could not comprehend his experience. Tai-Anh came to understand that what might be described as his experiences of cosmic consciousness could not only not be explained intellectually, they could not be comprehended intellectually.

Tai-Anh continued his training faithfully. One night he had a unique dream. In the dream, the sword that he always carried turned into a fragrant flower of vibrant colors. In the dream Tai-Anh met other people who were able to appreciate this miracle of transformation because they themselves were beings in the process of transforming themselves into persons who sought to discover all that is positive and precious in being alive, sentient, caring.

Tai-Anh awakened and realized that this dream would be the turning point in his life. A wonderful world of possibilities had appeared through the mysterious window of the dream, a world not perceived by the ordinary senses, but a phantasmagoria of immaterial substance of extraordinary beauty and indescribable radiance.

Tai-Anh's life changed completely following his dream. Remembering the wholesome discussions with his fellows during his student days, Tai-Anh began with renewed vigor to confirm in his everyday living a sense of his maturity, unity, harmony, and eternity. He no longer talked merely to keep a conversation alive. He no longer bent the truth to ease a personal or social awkwardness. Tai-Anh's self-quest became a quest for authenticity.

Some of Tai-Anh's students disliked the unwavering forthrightness which Tai-Anh now brought to all his lessons. In the months that followed, some of his most promising students left the school. Tai-Anh understood. They had been reared in a society oriented to objective understanding, to the rational rather than the emotional or spiritual. Everything for them had to be logical and quickly comprehensible or it could not become part of their reality.

Some of his students wanted to understand but had never been taught to be real, to be free. For those who stayed in training, Tai-Anh's unusual behavior, though it sometimes shocked them, also tended to jar them from some of their preconceptions and outmoded mental habits, as well as from the games they played with themselves and others.

Tai-Anh's glorious fulfillment was not, however, the end. It was only the beginning of an endless process of personal growth and spiritual transformation.

Ideals of justice, humanity, and conscience are the
duty of martial-arts practitioners.

Chapter 8

8

THE PATH OF DUTY

This is the way for those who want to learn my
    strategy:

Do not think dishonestly.

The Way is in the training itself.

Become acquainted with every art.

Know the Ways of all professions.

Distinguish between gain and loss in worldly
    matters.

Develop intuitive judgment and understanding for
    everything.

Perceive those things which cannot be seen.

Pay attention even to trifles.

Do nothing which is of no use.

                    —Miyamoto Musashi

A BOAT was sailing downstream on the Perfume River.
Among the passengers a man suddenly shouted at the
top of his lungs, "All of you stay where you are and
don't make a move or we'll throw you into the river!"

Eyes wide in fear, the passengers turned as one
toward the voice in the shadows to see a bandit bent on
accomplishing his wicked deed. With a rusty sword
raised over his head, he screamed a finishing note to his
threat. "Understood?"

The passengers stood as if turned to stone as four other bandits appeared here and there on the deck with weapons drawn. The outlaws systematically began stripping every passenger of money, earrings, necklaces, watches. Even sacks of food for the children were not spared. As a man of about fifty years of age was accosted, a bandit bellowed threateningly into his face, "Nothing to contribute?"

"Oh, yes. Something," the man replied and stood up slowly, fumbling through every pocket. To all appearances he was trying to find something to give to the bandit, when suddenly he loosed on the outlaw a volley of powerful blows. Striking and kicking with perfect precision, the erstwhile fumbler whisked the sword from the bandit's hand, turned and snatched the bag of loot from the grasp of another bandit, and tossed the sack to the deck amidst the passengers. Turning his complete attention to the bandits, he then attacked them in an astonishing display of mindful purpose and swordsmanship.

The passengers, faces locked in concern for the life of their rescuer, watched the drama unfold. Beyond the power of imagination of any of them, the lone swordsman, with amazing fighting skill, defeated all five bandits, one after another. The rescuer was none other than Tai-Anh.

Now in complete submission on the deck and binding their wounds under the victor's watchful control, the outlaws cast plainly admiring glances at Tai-Anh and spoke among themselves of the speed and gracefulness of their vanquisher. Tai-Anh called for the boat to dock and at the landing herded the limping five off to shore. The passengers crowded at the slip, much relieved but disappointed at not being able to express their heartfelt gratitude to Tai-Anh, watching him and the outlaws disappear quickly into the nearby village. A clang of the boat's bell, the raising of its sails, and the boat resumed its placid down-river voyage.

A few days later, at home in the city after a long absence, Tai-Anh visited a nearby inn where an elderly gentleman approached him saying, "Good afternoon, sir. I was one of the passengers whom you saved from robbers on the river last week. It is my pleasure to be able to express my appreciation and admiration for your work in saving us. The other passengers and I were sorely disappointed that we could not properly express our thanks for saving our lives and property with your exquisite martial skill."

"You praise me far beyond my deserving," replied Tai-Anh with a smile. "I did but what was necessary. We cannot close our eyes to such victimization and violence perpetrated on ourselves or on others. I simply did my duty."

"Duty to whom?" queried the old man.

"To the ideal of justice, I would say," responded Tai-Anh. "To humanity. To conscience. Just look about you," continued Tai-Anh with gentle gestures and a pained expression. "Everywhere we turn we see poverty, homelessness. Violence surrounds us. Attacks on the elderly and the disabled occur in broad daylight.

The safety and well-being of the children and the community as a whole are threatened at every turn.

"The threads which bind us together as civilized people, as a nation, are unraveling; but the leaders never even acknowledge this sorry state of ours. Our National Leader doesn't seem to care much, or is not accurately informed of the real situation. Well, perhaps he is engrossed in chasing his personal illusions, fame and fortune. We who practice the martial way, however, must follow through on our responsibilities, even if our leaders remain imprisoned in their houses of mirrors."

"Are there many of you practitioners of martial art doing this work?" the old man inquired with great courtesy.

"Martial artists are bound to lead simple and retiring lives; it is therefore difficult to identify who or where they are at any moment," Tai-Anh replied. "No one knows until some disaster occurs, and practitioners emerge to provide stability and assist the people. As the martial arts are flourishing, we may guess there must be a good many such men."

Tai-Anh's graceful and calmly knowledgeable demeanor caused the old man to feel an immediate affection for him, even a certain reverence. He said to Tai-Anh, "You are right. Those men occupy themselves with *The Way* and not merely with making a living. I not only admire them, but I'm also longing to meet more of them." The old man then invited Tai-Anh to his residence. Tai-Anh accepted the invitation at once, and the old man expressed his joy with the words, "Wonderful! Wonderful!"

As they strolled they reached the presidential palace, and the old man asked Tai-Anh to follow him in. The palace guards saluted the old man and made way for the two to pass into the palace. It dawned on Tai-Anh that the old man he accompanied on this leisurely stroll was none other than the President himself, disguised in common clothing.

"Please forgive me, Mr. President. I seem to have eyes without pupils or I would have recognized you at once." The President smiled and asked Tai-Anh not to be formal with him. Tai-Anh responded with a smile and an informal greeting.

That evening the banquet to welcome the President home from his journey included a ceremony to honor Tai-Anh's work in rescuing the sailing party. During the festivities, the President read a mandate officially recognizing Tai-Anh's good work and proposed that his rescuer assume the highest and most prestigious position on the presidential staff, that of National Teacher.

Though deeply honored, Tai-Anh respectfully declined the offer. "Mr. President, there are many learned and talented citizens in our country. I beg you to re-examine this favor that you wish to bestow upon me, for despite some gray hair I am not yet a mature person of great wisdom and mindfulness, and lack the qualifications to assume such a high position."

The President responded, "You may not have

attained the great age usual for that position, but remember that talent does not wait for age. I have found in you a virtuous and well-educated person, and my choice is not based upon age. Master Tai-Anh please do not cause me despair!"

On the one hand Tai-Anh had always thought that positions of honor and great riches were the very stuff of egomania and selfishness. But as he reflected on the President's plea for help in guiding the nation, he wondered whether rejecting the opportunity to serve the people was just as prejudiced and self-indulgent. Perhaps one must occasionally rely on positions of leadership and power to be able to help others, Tai-Anh thought to himself. One of the fundamental principles of martial art is gaining without gladness and losing without sadness. Abstaining from matters from which others cannot abstain and performing deeds that others cannot perform are the business of the martial-arts practitioner.

Thinking so, Tai-Anh at last humbly accepted the honor, and all the guests applauded his decision. The President expressed his own hearty contentment by means of his grand and majestic smile, and awarded Tai-Anh the golden presidential seal.

Arrogance has made him a mere servant.

Chapter 9

9

WEAVING THE WEB
OF KARMA

With your right hand
Showing yang,
Your left hand showing yin,
Lead your opponent.

—Morihei Ueshiba

HAVING ASSUMED his new eminence as National
Teacher, Master Tai-Anh remained in the palace for
some time, helping the President to reorganize and
strengthen the defense of the nation and to bring the
administrative body toward greater service to the
people. As time passed and Tai-Anh's influence was felt
more and more in the halls of government, children no
longer fell to hunger and disease. New schools were
opened. Men and women walked city streets and
country roads pridefully, with a sense of peace, and
without fear of violence.

Though Master Tai-Anh's reputation had risen to
great heights among the Presidential staff and elsewhere in the city, his mind and heart were mostly with
the people of the country. Living a luxurious, powerful,
and publicly influential life was exciting, but not at all

an important part of Master Tai-Anh's nature. Again and again he sought permission to return to his previous life, but each time the President cited a pressing need for Tai-Anh's continuing service.

One day Tai-Anh received the President's consent that he might leave the government to travel among the people, but on condition that he return within five years or whenever the country was in time of need. The President was downhearted at Master Tai-Anh's decision to leave, but understood Tai-Anh's need to be among people he loved so deeply. The President dispatched a dozen guards to escort the National Teacher and ordered a large supply of goods to accompany them wherever Tai-Anh directed.

With great courtesy Tai-Anh declined the President's generous offer, observing that such complex arrangements would be an unwarranted expense to the President and the nation and would actually interfere with Tai-Anh's intended goals. The President, recalling the benefits of his own incognito trips, was impressed yet again and doubly sad at Tai-Anh's departure. The next morning Tai-Anh slipped out of the palace alone, leaving behind all the gifts and retainers and supplies.

Tai-Anh went directly to the distant place to which he had taken the five outlaws captured on the boat some time before. That place was not the police station, as the passengers might have assumed at the time; it was instead Tai-Anh's school where, after promising Tai-Anh to seek a new life, the outlaws had been installed as students. The outlaws had been not only impressed by Tai-Anh's prowess with the sword, they had been fascinated as well by the loving kindness and the pure-heartedness communicated by this powerful but gentle man. As time passed and the former thugs applied themselves to study as they had promised, the five outlaws became saturated with Tai-Anh's own mystic power.

Year after year, the school attracted large numbers of martial-arts practitioners who came to study with Tai-Anh and the five former outlaws. Master Tai-Anh was especially pleased the day that the former outlaws were ordained into the Martial Way. A significant transformation had occurred, changing beasts into men, murderers into citizens. The five bandits had become five gentlemen.

Master Tai-Anh continued on the path of duty. One morning, remembering the promise he had made to the President to return to government service within five years, Tai-Anh realized that the time had come. He would return now to his work as National Teacher. Bidding farewell to all the students and teachers, Master Tai-Anh boarded a fine old sailing vessel and headed for the capital.

The National Teacher was wiping some spray from his eyeglasses when a young man found a small space next to him and sat down.

"Where are you bound, my young friend?" National Teacher Tai-Anh, smiling pleasantly, asked the young man.

In a loud voice and an ostentatious manner the youth replied, "I am going to the capital to take the national government examination."

"Well, good luck to you. I wish you success," said Tai-Anh with warmth.

Looking down his nose at Tai-Anh's modest garb and unprepossessing demeanor, the student laughed and in a sarcastic tone asked the National Teacher, "Are you on a business trip?"

Ignoring the tone and the sneering attitude, Tai-Anh replied, "No, I am the National Teacher, and I am returning to the service of the President."

The young man snorted. "What? The President invited you? Do you take me for a fool?" Master Tai-Anh was silent as the youth continued. "Don't make me laugh, old man. The President would no more honor you as National Teacher than he would the man in the moon!"

"Why do you insult me?" Master Tai-Anh asked mildly. "You asked me a question, and I answered you honestly, but all you do in return is sneer at me. I don't understand."

The young man shot back, "Do you expect me to believe that you are such a worthy and enlightened individual? Ha! A National Teacher must be a distinguished person who has an imposing figure, is luxuriously dressed in the most fashionable clothes, and is surrounded by an entourage of adoring people. You are none of these. You pretend to such an honorable title, but your appearance gives you away."

"Whether or not you believe me does not truly matter," Master Tai-Anh replied. He thought a moment, chuckled to himself, and continued. "In a barrel of fish eyes one does not often see the pearl."

This reply incensed the young man who, with rising voice and darkening face said, "Fish eyes? A pearl? You're an impostor! Look at yourself, cloaked in common clothing, no guards, no retainers, no badges of distinction. And you pretend to be such a person as the National Teacher!" The young man drew himself up to full height and pronounced expansively, "If you are who you claim to be. I volunteer to serve you for free."

"Ah!" said Master Tai-Anh quickly. "For how long! Two or three months perhaps?"

"For three full years," the young man said grandly, so that all could hear.

"You won't fall back on your promise?"

"Never!" replied the brash youth. "And what happens if you're not who you claim to be? What then?"

"Oh, I would serve you for the rest of my life," Master Tai-Anh replied. The two barely smiled at one another. The bet was on.

Such are the webs of karma we weave for ourselves, for even as they agreed to wager, it was an agreement to engage in a spiritual combat. The young man believed Master Tai-Anh to be lying and wanted only to catch the old man in the bluff to teach Old Fish-Eye a lesson. Master Tai-Anh, on the other hand, was quietly amused at the arrogance of the sharp-edged young man. Tai-Anh rejoiced at the opportunity to teach the youngster not to scorn and insult elders. The snake of karma had begun to curl.

Next day, as the sun broke through the morning mist, the boat pulled into port, and Master Tai-Anh and the young man took the road to the capital. They spoke not at all. As they approached the capital, however, the student noticed that Master Tai-Anh seemed to grow in dignity and refinement, even appearing to become taller with every passing mile. Sensing these changes, the young man became nervous. As they approached the palace, passing citizens smiled and bowed when they recognized Master Tai-Anh, and the young man realized he may have made a major error in judgment.

As the two entered the palace, the President, surprised and elated at Tai-Anh's return, greeted his National Teacher with a deep bow and immediately ordered preparations for a welcoming banquet.

Thanking the President for his kind greeting, the National Teacher said, "Mr. President, this young man is named Lam. He has volunteered to serve me as an attendant for three years."

The President was pleased to hear of this devotion and thereupon made the bargain official by ordering Lam to serve the National Teacher diligently. Lam felt as if the blood had drained from his body. He appeared pale and small, his head lowered in shame. He nodded his understanding and willingness to obey.

Lam served the National Teacher for three years, but not happily. He continually grieved the loss of his dreams, so full of grand hopes and powerful fantasies. Now he had become a mere servant, and this fall made him feel disgraced and disgusted with his life. Lam had not yet learned that honest work is right work.

In time Lam appeared to overcome his pretentiousness. He performed well his duties as servant. He found that the role became easier to play as time passed, and no one ever suspected that he was full of rage and resentment. Master Tai-Anh provided Lam with all material support during the three years, provided many opportunities for Lam to learn the secrets of leadership, and even helped Lam's family at times. Still, Lam remained disgruntled.

Feeling once again the urge to return to the country and the people, Master Tai-Anh decided to release Lam from service. "Do you still want to become a government official?" Master Tai-Anh asked Lam.

"Yes, sir," replied Lam. "I came here three years ago to live up to my stupid bargain to serve you, but I still do nourish an earnest desire to serve the people through a career in government."

"Have you learned what are the important qualities of a leader?" Master Tai-Anh queried.

"Yes, of course. The important duties are patriotism and . . . and . . . er . . . to serve and to love the people," Lam parroted.

Discerning the lack of sincerity in Lam's words and knowing something of Lam's weaknesses, Master Tai

Anh nevertheless believed that all humans are creatures of conscience. He would give Lam his chance. "Being a leader does require that you be loyal and patriotic and that you love and diligently serve the people. Yes, these are all certainly true! But in addition to these, a leader must cultivate himself. This means you need to train yourself in compassion, ethics, and honesty in order for you to be able to create a healthy and compassionate society. And self-cultivation requires that you develop mindfulness and seriousness and respect for each and every living being."

"I will be able to fulfill all these requirements," Lam insisted.

Master Tai-Anh continued. "Remember that our words, feelings, thoughts, and deeds must travel the same path at the same time. If there is something you wish to accomplish in this life, you must get in touch with your true feelings and thoughts before you act. Contemplate again and again; and if such a proposed act is associated with ego, delusion, or ill-will or is conducive to harming another, then that is a dark deed, a bad deed. Avoid it. If, on the other hand, there is something you wish to accomplish which is associated with no-ego, with good-will, and is conducive to the benefit of another, then this is a bright deed, a good deed. Do it! Do it without becoming tired of it."

Shooing a moth through the partially opened window, the National Teacher placed his hand on Lam's shoulder and said, "Do not allow yourself a single thought or feeling or action that could be harmful to others because, as you have learned in these three years, a person who seeks to harm another person—or who is able but neglects to protect one who requires protection—that person must harvest all the consequences of those actions."

Master Tai-Anh looked intently at Lam, awaiting a response and receiving none. Lam stood still, his eyes shining, his thoughts on the possibilities in officialdom. After a few moments, the National Teacher left the room and secured a position for Lam as chief of a small district which lay far to the north of the capital. Lam was ecstatic when he learned of the appointment. He envisioned all his old dreams finally coming true.

Master Tai-Anh provided Lam with the opportunity to put himself to the test even though Tai-Anh suspected that Lam was not yet ready to absorb the insights he offered, insights which had been transmitted from teacher to disciple throughout the ages. Sometimes the teachings fall on fertile ground, sometimes not. Sometimes impulses within us which are truly fundamental require that we repeat the same mistake again and again until suddenly one day we see our folly clearly and change our ways. Master Tai-Anh had reminded himself of these truths as he arranged for Lam to become chief of Tai-Anh's own home district.

As a district chief in a remote area of the state, Lam enjoyed all kinds of freedom. He was free to choose the path of compassion and love or the path of arrogance and brutality. Once again, Lam chose the snaked path. At first Lam dared show no sign of a rebellious or arrogant attitude. Gradually, however, he learned that the mere symbols of his new office could dampen people's resistance to his haughty ways. Even when people became deeply dissatisfied with his operations, even when he knew that the people felt victimized, Lam simply instituted the brutal law of his own fantasies, pursuing his personal goal of transforming the community school of martial arts into an equestrian center.

The resident teachers and students of the school vigorously resisted this gross change in direction, and Lam's power was tested. But as he had absolute authority, Lam simply expelled the teachers and all the practitioners, and began the process of remodeling the school. He was pleased with his actions. He was pleased with himself. The people of the district, however, were shocked, dumfounded by the mindless cruelty of this man who had worked in close service to Master Tai-Anh, the highly respected National Teacher.

Lam had forgotten a principal admonition about karma: the corrupting quality of power; for when he was within his own domain and possessed complete and total power over the people, he exercised that power enthusiastically to honor and nourish his own ego. But karma is not a simple chain of cause-and-effect. Karma is more like the web of the spider which, when a thread is touched, vibrates to every one of its farthest corners.

The web of karma is broken.

Chapter 10

The Web is Broken

The frogs fall silent
Ceasing all their argument:
Someone's on the bridge.

—Ryoto

At the very moment when Lam decided to destroy the martial-arts school, Master Tai-Anh, sitting far away in the stillness of meditation, sensed disturbing movement within. Intuition told him that a misfortune was about to occur somewhere, and that the misfortune was related to Master Tai-Anh's life. He walked out of the presidential palace without a fixed destination.

At the Perfume River, an old woman on a boat waved to the master and handed him an envelope upon which had been scrawled in a familiar hand one simple line: "Please come at once to your school in the Northern District." Master Tai-Anh knew at once that this was an urgent message from one of his teachers. He hurried to the north.

As Tai-Anh approached the gate of the school, the whole picture of this very familiar place revived in his memory. He recalled the many months spent with students in caring for the school, painting window shutters, mending arbors in the orchard, feeding the goldfish and carp in the central fountain. But the school now was evidently empty, desolate. Master Tai-Anh saw a young woman sitting beside the still and empty fountain, apparently deeply grieving.

"Dear child, I see no teachers and students anywhere. What has happened here?" Master Tai-Anh inquired.

The young woman stared at the master for a moment and answered in a sorrowful voice. "The teachers and students have been expelled by Chief Lam, and tomorrow that evil man will be here to demolish this beautiful old martial-arts school and build in its place a school for horsemen. We have tried to resist this oppression, but the district chief has power in weapons and in assistants who are just like him."

Tai-Anh was stupefied upon hearing this news. He found it difficult to believe that the same Lam he had tutored as his attendant and awarded the title of Chief of District was now the leader of a gang of thugs.

"Would you please describe this person named Lam?" Master Tai-Anh asked the young woman.

"We have heard that he once was a close attendant to Master Tai-Anh, the National Teacher." She paused. "If that is true, they should both go to hell. Any National Teacher that would support such a monster is a disgrace. I am too young to have mastered the Martial Way, and there is little hope of my meeting the National Teacher, otherwise I would risk my life against both of them for what they have done to us and to this school," she said passionately.

Master Tai-Anh shared with the young student that Lam's plan would be terminated. Chief Lam would be ordered to refurbish and embellish the school. The young woman quickly understood that the person before her was the National Teacher himself, evidently very much concerned with what he saw, and she immediately apologized for her discourteous manner, agreeing to help in setting up a small hut in the middle of the square in front of the school. When the hut was completed, Tai-Anh hand-lettered a small sign to hang over the doorway. The sign read, "The National Teacher Is Here."

The next morning Master Tai-Anh sat alone in the hut waiting for Lam. At about ten o'clock, a group of fifty soldiers with pick-axes and shovels advanced toward the school. Lam was in the forefront, riding grandly in a long carriage carried by four robust soldiers.

Seeing the hut in the middle of the square, Lam was outraged. He jumped down, ax in hand, prepared to raze the shed with his own hands. Then he read the sign on the hut and saw the National Teacher sitting in deep meditation at the entrance.

Lam was thunderstruck. In a flash he recognized that his entire tenure as district chief had been an exercise in arrogant self-indulgence, and that he was now in grave trouble. Signaling his soldiers to follow his lead, Lam fell to his knees and bowed his head to the ground as all the soldiers stood like statues, gazing at their previously overbearing district chief in wide-eyed disbelief. Then

Master Tai-Anh ordered Lam to come closer and reprimanded him sternly, but in a soft voice that only Lam could hear. "Lam, you are a selfish, arrogant ingrate, a power-crazed and unreliable person. Do you remember my words to you when I conferred on you this position of trust years ago? Do you?"

"Yes, Your Excellency. I do remember," Lam replied.

"Then, what of all this?" said Master Tai-Anh, waving a hand to indicate the vacant buildings and the military work detail. Lam began to bang his head against the ground, quaking in fear. "Please forgive me, Your Excellency. I beg your pardon. I beg your mercy. I pledge never to commit such deeds again."

"Is that all you have to say?" Master Tai-Anh asked.

"I pledge to repair the school, to make it even more beautiful and magnificent than it ever was," Lam pleaded.

"And at whose expense?" Master Tai-Anh queried.

"All expenses will be my own," Lam replied. In order to alleviate part of Lam's bad karma, Master Tai-Anh agreed to the proposal regarding the repairs, and then asked again, "Is that all?"

"No, Master," Lam replied. "There is more, for I must heal myself, rid myself of this poisonous arrogance and selfishness. I will take leave and spend the rest of my life in study and contemplation. I will study the *Tao* and nurture the balanced approach to reason as you have always instructed me to do. I will sit in the stillness of meditation—forever, if need be—or until I touch the deeper well of my spirituality and intuitive consciousness and can arise knowing that I am a person of love and compassion." That afternoon, Lam returned with all the soldiers and began the restoration of the school. The work proceeded rapidly and the repairs were completed in a matter of weeks.

Not long after that part of the restoration was accomplished, Lam was preparing himself to be demoted in rank and transferred to a small far-away district. But as Lam had deliberately determined to change and improve his life, the National Teacher permitted him to stay. "You are not to be transferred to another district, Lam. You are no longer an official of the government, but I will allow you to remain here to study, at this school under my complete supervision."

The students and teachers who had already returned to the school were shocked to think that Chief Lam, who only weeks before had thrown them from their beloved school and had laid plans to demolish it, would now be a student at the school. Lam's face was bathed in anxious perspiration as he glanced around the crowd of students standing in the square. In that moment, Lam came to truly understand the law of karma that reminds us that as we sow our seeds to the wind, we must ultimately reap the whirlwind of consequences. Every infringement of the immutable laws of karma must be paid for somewhere, sometime, sooner or later. For Lam, the time was now.

Aikido is not techniques to fight with or defeat the enemy. It is the way to reconcile the world and make human beings one family.

Chapter 11

The First Lesson

> When I teach my Way, I first teach by training
> in techniques which are easy for the pupil to
> understand, a doctrine which is easy to under-
> stand. I gradually endeavor to explain the deep
> principle.
>
> —Miyamoto Musashi

MASTER TAI-ANH escorted Lam to the large training room. As they entered, Lam was impressed with its new feeling of spaciousness. The immense surface was now matted with canvas padded with a mixture of sawdust and shredded rubber, a firm yet yielding practice ground.

Master Tai-Anh motioned Lam to a room next to the training area where meditation pillows were placed neatly before a low table on which was an incense-burner and a vase containing multicolored flowers. "This is where each day's training will begin for you, in silent meditation on the essence of *The Way*. Here is where you must study and cultivate the martial way and submit to the *Tao*. Understood?" Master Tai-Anh spoke thus to Lam even though he knew that Lam was ignorant of the meaning.

"Yes, Your Excellency!" Lam answered reflexively as

he glanced over the heads of a number of students sitting in silent meditation.

Master Tai-Anh led Lam to another room next to the meditation hall where stood long racks containing various training instruments. As they passed each variety of instrument, Master Tai-Anh pronounced its name. "Here is the lance, the dagger, the double-hook sword, the broadsword, short-staff, long-staff, two-section staff, three-section staff, nine-section chain, sickle. Look, here are Japanese *bokken*, *tanto*, *jo*. You will someday know these instruments as though they were your own appendages, extensions of your own body-mind-spirit."

Then both moved to the far side of the training room where a number of male and female students stood motionless, performing their *ch'i-kung* exercises, as on the other side of the room a dozen old and young persons moved through their *t'ai-chi ch'uan* routine in front of large-mirrored walls. All seemed totally unaware of the intrusion of Master Tai-Anh and Lam and behaved as though they were in a sort of suspended animation.

Lam's face shone with amazement at this incredible place with its concurrent serenity and ceaseless activity of the many students vigorously practicing their art or sitting quietly meditating in the midst of this activity. Signalling Lam to sit on a mat, Master Tai-Anh informed him, "You will begin your training tomorrow. Although I must return to the presidential palace, I will instruct each of your teachers on how your training is to unfold, and I will remain in communication with each of them throughout the process."

Master Tai-Anh paused, staring deeply into Lam's eyes. "In addition, I will of course surprise you with visits myself and check on the progress of your training from time to time. Is this understood?" "Yes, Your Excellency. This is all understood," Lam replied softly.

Before leaving, Master Tai-Anh added, "Perhaps when you have mastered the principles and philosophy underlying all martial art, you will be free of your old baggage."

Lam accompanied Master Tai-Anh to the main gate and made a formal bow. Then he returned to the training hall which was now empty of students. Lam savored the moment of quiet as he slowly surveyed the entire perimeter of the hall, knowing full well that he would spend many days and nights getting to know every square inch of this place, especially its matted floor.

And so, on the following morning, Lam's training did officially begin. Having completed his chores in the residence hall and his meditation, Lam was then engaged in a routine of *aiki* exercises *(aiki undo)* including many types of breakfalls *(ukemi)*.

Four weeks elapsed. One morning after a lengthy talk on some sort of theory and principles, the teacher asked Lam to hold one of her wrists with both his hands. The movement is known as a two-handed-grasp attack *(ryo te mochi)*. At first the teacher explained how to break the attacker's balance by using *ki*-energy.

Then she demonstrated this balance-breaking by means of a body "displacement" *(tai sabaki)* and then, extending her arm gently but firmly across Lam's front, completed a breath throw *(kokyu nage)*. The teacher exercised the technique, called *ryo te mochi kokyu nage*, simply and effortlessly. Lam teetered, lost his balance and fell to the mat.

As soon as Lam completed his recovery roll and came to a standing position, the teacher grasped Lam's wrist and asked him to perform the same technique. Lam tried hard but could not budge the teacher.

"Now, don't think that you have an opponent in front of you. I am not here," the teacher explained. "No one is here holding your wrist. If you do not ignore my presence then you will rely on your physical strength and try to subdue me physically. Remember that the ocean of energy *(ki no umi)* resides in your belly *(hara)* just below the navel. It is from there the mysterious *ki* emanates.

"You must cultivate the sensation, the feeling of bringing that energy up through your chest, through your shoulders, through your stretched arm, out your fingertips, and through that wall, hundreds of miles away. This firm action of course must be in harmony with the apparently loose *tai sabaki* I have just demonstrated. Now, try it!"

Lam clenched his jaw, tightened his shoulders and arms, attempting to overcome his teacher with the brute force of his much heavier and more muscularly powerful physique. Lam's body remained frozen in a great knot of strength, but all the effort resulted in failure, attempt after attempt.

The teacher repeated the previous remark saying, "Your body is too rigid, too stiff! How can a dead body move? Relax, Lam! Relax to allow *ki* to flow freely through you like water through a garden hose. Feel the flow!"

Lam closed his eyes, and took a deep breath, trying to be less tense, to release himself from his body's rigidity, stiffness, and anxiety. Oddly, Lam found after a number of times that he was less tired and more relaxed. Feeling his feet planted solidly but not fixed to the floor, Lam began to perform the *kokyu nage*, first with the teacher and then with fellow students.

At one point, a point he barely noticed, Lam slipped into an entirely new context, one that dealt with the qualities of blending, centering, and grounding his energy and yet extending it through space. As this aikido routine unfolded, it became clear to Lam that for a brief moment he had become more and more immersed in some sort of mysterious energy flow.

As he gained in confidence with his new success, he felt he needed to show off his understanding, saying, "I thought that whenever an attack is launched toward us, we are not to resist the attack, but draw it in, to accommodate it, just as the little willow tree accommodates the weight of the snow and the force of the wind. Then, at the appropriate moment, just a little momentum is applied and then all is well. We don't really have to be concerned with the *ki* in every moment, do we?"

The teacher looked at Lam and smiled. Lam grew quiet and appeared quite proud of his logical exposition which, perhaps, he had heard or read about somewhere.

The teacher nodded in agreement, replying, "Your observation is true in a way, Lam, because it fits with your rational and logical mind. However, beautiful as it may sound, your explanation is itself a trick, a theoretical trick designed by human intellect. Whether one is aware of one's embodiment each moment or only in special moments is a purely intellectual speculation. Any answer to the question would have to be based on some sort of theory, but the very fact of your being conscious of it turns it against you. Such theorizing is not natural at all. Do you believe that the beaver damming the stream or the bird flying in the sky works from some sort of theory about its existence? Does the beaver have a theory of engineering or the bird a theory of aeronautics? How about the honeycomb of the bee? Is that the product of the bee's thinking about it? All human tricks are artificial, not natural, Lam. And artificiality is not the *Tao*."

Seeing Lam's bewilderment with ontology, she continued, "I am not saying that what you have said is of no use whatsoever. I am saying that the *Tao* works to free the intellect and the senses. When you are free of the obstacles of the intellect, you are in union with nature. When your energy is in harmony with the energy of the universe, then wondrous experiences unfold."

Though confused, Lam gained some satisfaction from the teacher's elucidation. What he had said was "not of no use." Lam glowed inwardly with self-satisfaction and vowed to be assiduous in his training. His glow dimmed somewhat at her next words and he listened carefully.

"Lam, as one who is recovering from the disease of temporal power-hunger, you must be particularly alert to avoid the trap of appearance, a condition to which you may be especially susceptible. Unhappily, this valuing of appearance has been adopted by far too many martial-arts practitioners as the fulcrum of their activities and livelihood. The operant axiom of such people is display, exhibition, and combat for the win-at-any-price. The empty but tempting formula of appearance fails to even recognize, much less to understand, the fundamental principle of life. It leads to disaster. You must resolve to refuse any such temptation.

"Remember the words of the Master, 'The true martial way is not technique to fight with or defeat the enemy. It is the way to reconcile the world and make human beings one family.' Lam, the art which you are now addressing, aikido, is not a weapon to lead the world into conflict and destruction. Aikido is a way of harmonizing with the *Tao* in order to attain deliverance. This harmonizing must be the purpose of your training."

"Ah," said Lam.

But at this point, Lam was simply a novice. He could

not so soon fathom the truth that however advanced in the mastery of theory and technique, the martial-arts practitioner is only a slave to delusions without recognizing that the essence of one's fighting artistry lies in one's loving and compassionate nature.

The proper purpose of martial-arts training is training
the body, cultivating the mind, so as to nurture the
spirit and contribute to the welfare of the world.

Chapter 12

LAM HAS ANOTHER
LESSON

One man boasted, "My bow is so good, it needs no arrow!" Another man boasted, "My arrow is so good, it needs no bow." The skilled archer Le heard them and said, "Without a bow, how can you shoot an arrow? And without an arrow, how can you hit the target?" So the bow and the arrow were used together, and Le taught these men to shoot.

—Ch'en Fu

LAM TRAINED long and hard in various disciplines—kung-fu, judo, aikido, t'ai-chi ch'uan—and began to nurture the dream of becoming a grand champion, making his name well known. Equipped with all the special techniques of competition and a strong confidence in his strength and youthfulness, Lam now desired fervently to bring his dream into reality.

One day, when Lam expressed to the judo teacher his idea of touring the country and competing in tournaments, the teacher looked at him and burst out laughing. Lam was both wounded and outraged. "Teacher, don't you trust my ability? After all, I have defeated all the highest caliber students in the school!"

The teacher was watching Hau, a student of Lam's age, who was sweeping the training hall. "Ah, Lam. But you have not done what you think." Pointing at Hau, he said, "Lam, if you win in competition with Hau, in any discipline you choose, then you may undertake the trip across the country engaging in your contests. But if you lose, you will have to take over Hau's duties for many long months. What do you say?"

Lam smiled to himself, thinking that this would be really easy, for he knew Hau's skill very well. Lam cheerfully accepted the teacher's proposition, but the outcome of the trial was disastrous for Lam. He lost three consecutive combats to Hau, felt humiliated, and became depressed. Quite unexpectedly, the teacher said, "Although you have lost the competition, I will let you make the trip, Lam, but you must come back here within three years. Agreed?" With great relief and joy, Lam agreed and took his leave of the school.

Nearly three years later, the pursuit of the dream had shaped Lam into a tough, experienced, and invincible combatant. Lam returned to the school to see the judo teacher, to exhibit to his fellow students the many techniques and trophies he had gained—and, of course, to display his combative superiority, especially against Hau.

Strangely, however, in combat against Hau, Lam once again could not last more than a few minutes. Lam found this unbelievable. Not only that, but other students, one after another, swept over Lam as well. Lam was exhausted and bewildered, embarrassed beyond belief.

"You have indeed made the progress you sought during the past three years," the teacher whispered to Lam, "but as you see, the kind of progress you believed would advance you, has not advanced you anywhere at all. You are still pursuing the outer, but not getting the inside yet. Your mind is still busy with accumulating techniques and tricks, with winning and losing, with name and fame. Such is not the proper aim of martial-arts training. Its purpose must be the training of the body and the cultivating of the mind so as to nurture the spirit and to contribute in some way to the welfare of the world's people. These are the ultimate aims in the training of martial arts, and judo is no exception."

While the teacher confided these truths, Lam's mind wandered elsewhere, perhaps thinking of his recent shameful defeats. Noticing that dispirited attitude, the teacher asked, "Are you listening, Lam?"

"Yes, yes, Teacher," stammered Lam.

"You said you are listening, but it is evident to me that you are not, Lam. When you listen to me with your ears alone, you are not really listening. If you want to truly understand me, do not try to understand intellectually. Rather, listen to me with your heart. Understand me with the feeling that speaks to you inside yourself."

The teacher paused a minute or so and continued. "I have given you years in which to travel and grow, hoping this period would provide an opportunity for you to work toward the inside of your being. But you are still browsing on the superficial. Your ego is still invested in your demonstration of powerful movements and spectacular tricks. But when it comes to reality, you cannot stand more than three minutes with any of it." Lam stood motionless and listened.

The teacher continued. "The reason for all of this is that your mind is too restless, too much focused on the façade of your self. As long as you remain fixed on the appearance of your being, you will be unable to make real progress. Unless you find your center, unless you penetrate inwards, you will continue to lose your balance. Lam, you are not growing and you will not grow. All your effort becomes futile.

Ashamed of the bitter defeats he had just suffered, as well as this rebuke by the teacher, Lam asked softly, "How shall I know myself? How can I go into the center of my being?"

"When I explain something to you, Lam, don't try to listen only intellectually. You will be unable to understand then, because you are then conscious only of my words and distracted by mental activity. At such times you are never within. And because you are never within your body and within its feelings and within its emotions, you are never able to get to the heart of any matter!"

Motioning Lam to the mat, the teacher said, "To get beneath the words themselves, to contact the heart of all meaning, you must experience the here-and-now, here and now." With those words, he and Lam spontaneously broke into free practice *(randori)*. Both whirled around with attacks, defenses, counterattacks. Suddenly, Lam was thrown on the mat by a fantastic body-drop technique *(tai otoshi)*, then thrown a second time by a left inner-thigh throw *(hidari uchi mata)*, then by a hip sweep *(harai goshi)*. Barely risen from the mat for the third time, Lam was sent in the air again by a wonderful shoulder wheel *(kata guruma)*.

In a few brief moments and in spite of all his effort, Lam had been thrown four times. After struggling to his feet after the fourth fall, he attempted many hard attacks but simply could not budge the teacher who simply rooted himself solidly on the mat or, just as simply and lightly as a feather, floated high and dodged each of Lam's offenses, beautifully and effectively demonstrating the way of flexibility *(ju no ri)*.

"This is becoming more serious than a workout," Lam thought. Then, with his own special shoulder throw *(seoi nage)*, Lam sent the teacher flying over his head. But like a cat, the latter curved his back agilely while in the air and landed softly on his feet. With incredible suddenness, the teacher emitted a powerful *kiai* (vocalized energy) as he performed a spring hip *(hane goshi)*, lifting Lam from the mat and sending him soaring through the air.

The moment Lam's body slammed into contact with the mat, the teacher immobilized him with a simple but powerful shoulder pin *(kata gatame)*. As the mat work *(ne waza)* phase began, Lam, sweating and breathless, struggled desperately to free himself, but all his struggles were in vain. He was unable to move, almost unable to breathe. "That's enough. Please! Enough!" Lam pleaded.

The teacher loosened his grip and said, "Well, Lam, your external tricks appear strong, but your *ki* is powerless. It is rudderless. Your balance breaking *(kuzushi)* is awkward. Your mind is stiff. You are obsessed with throwing me while you yourself are afraid of being thrown." The teacher knelt and smoothed his practice garment while Lam wiped the perspiration from his face. "I haven't seen you work like this before," Lam said.

"Before the time is not the time. After the time is no longer time. When the time is, it is time," the teacher quoted with a smile and continued. "Have you ever questioned why I permitted you to go on a tour even after you lost to Hau?" "I wondered about that," Lam replied, "but I decided that you thought I was, in a way, ready to bring honor and fame to the school."

The teacher remained silent for a moment and then said, sternly, "So. That is what you thought. Hm. Well, here is what I think, Lam. I think now is the time for you to take over Hau's duty. Perhaps all your problems will yet be solved."

And so Lam, feeling belittled and confused, took on the chores of a simple student once again. Spending long hours daily sweeping the huge mat and performing menial tasks in the school gave Lam time to ponder the situation he had created for himself. He recalled what his teacher had told him: that his mind was stiff and overly concerned with opposing others, with winning, with showing-off; and that he was afraid of being thrown and of losing. Slowly Lam came to realize how this mind-set is bound to reinforce ignorance of the true art. Such a mind leads to presumption and pretension which eventually stop the fluidity of one's movements and interfere with one's spiritual development. Lam began to transform himself.

Month after month, with disciplined practice and the close guidance of his teacher, Lam gained more calmness and poise in his attitude, and in his freedom and fluidity of movement. His technique moved into a new form of adaptability and appropriateness. He became more able to move from one state into another in a fusion of the real and the unreal without interference from his thinking processes. Many months passed and the teacher, noting the powerful growth that Lam was making toward perfection as a martial artist, as a human being, transferred him to another section for further training.

Sometimes the master cries while others laugh and
laughs while others cry.

Chapter 13

ON THE PURSUIT OF CREATIVITY

Zhu Pingman went to the eminent butcher Zhili Yi
to learn how to carve dragons for the table. He
studied for more than three years and spent all
his very considerable property before he mastered the subject. But he never found a dragon on
which to practice his art.

—Zhuang Zi

SEVERAL YEARS into Lam's training, Master Tai-Anh
made another in a long series of visits to the school.
The Master was requested to give a special seminar to
a select group of teachers, and Lam was assigned to
handle the appropriate protocol for the event.

After the first day of the seminar, several teachers
came to Master Tai-Anh to show their appreciation.
One said, "Master, it was an excellent seminar day, and
we enjoyed your techniques very much. Thank you."
Another said, "Today's techniques were fabulous. We
have never experienced such techniques before. Thank
you for sharing your knowledge with us." The third
person expressed similar sentiments, saying, "Master,
how long does it take to be able to perform those

127

spectacular and effective counterattacks?" Others from the group were equally effusive in their praise for Master Tai-Anh's techniques.

Master Tai-Anh appeared disappointed. Noticing this behavior, one senior teacher asked, "Master Tai-Anh, it seems you are not happy that those teachers praised you so highly." Master Tai-Anh replied calmly, "I must have done something improper, something wrong. Otherwise, how could those men and women have enjoyed it so much? They have expressed their satisfaction, their joy, over my techniques. What techniques did I demonstrate to them? I must have shown something wrong."

This ambiguous reply is in fact very clear to those who have a reverent mind, a mind that seeks the source of beauty and hidden technique, a mind that searches for the internal, the nucleus of things. The martial artist must always remember that shows of fabulous technique are only expressions of the forms created and given substance from within and manifested through a divine mind. That point is the essence of the seminar that the teachers failed to capture. They failed to grasp the Master's real intent, for they had allowed their habits to become oriented to appearance, to surface phenomena, to social lubrication. They had not taken the trouble to look for and question the origin of those many beautiful and unique techniques and insights. Instead, they had allowed themselves to become fascinated with the beautiful surface reflections, with transient and fleeting appearances which come and go like the wispy clouds on the windswept peaks of mountains.

How could the Master manifest satisfaction with the gracious but childish response of the teachers when it had become painfully evident to him that none of them had grasped the message he brought? That message had become worthless. Master Tai-Anh could not show satisfaction; he could instead have wept. As the old saying goes, "Sometimes the Master cries while others laugh, and laughs while others cry." This adage summarizes well the whole seminar.

One should realize that all designed techniques and ready-made thoughts are considered to spring from very unsophisticated needs, and that accommodation to these needs is essential only for newcomers to the martial arts. Because they are shallow, superficial, external like the bark of a tree, ready-made thoughts and techniques are virtually unacceptable for advanced practitioners—the teachers. Much of that bark is likely to fall away and disintegrate over time, whereas the sap, the vital circulating fluid under the bark, continues to nourish the growth and development of the tree.

Authentic practitioners of the martial arts work so diligently on their inner selves because they know that all the outer self does is respond to the inner. Thus, the intrinsic nature, the basic substance, the necessary constituent that gives birth to the whole course of flowing movement emanates from within the being. One's deep awareness of the body within itself is the source of one's spiritual awakening. This is the essential point that all the teachers at the seminar had ignored. Only when this one point is understood may a thousand other movements grow accordingly; misunderstand it, and ten thousand delusions will arise and demand attention.

During the remainder of the seminar, Master Tai-Anh felt it was necessary to provide a new approach to the training, guiding the participants to be more aware of this critical point. Otherwise, the teachers would teach like the blind leading the blind. Otherwise they would all fall into the same trap, the pit of ignorance. They were falling but they did not know they were falling. That was the problem Master Tai-Anh had identified.

At the end of the seminar one of Master Tai-Ahn's veteran students raised an issue that had been at the forefront of the Master's mind.

"Master," the student began, "for more than two decades I have been teaching the art. Most of the advanced techniques I taught were of my creation. I was happy and proud of that creativity. I was satisfied with my teaching and with the progress of my students—until yesterday, when in a few moments you rendered all my attacks useless. I spent all last night pondering this absolute defeat. I cannot understand how I could have become all at once so ineffectual. Please help me comprehend my problem."

The Master, who was ready to unveil additional training mysteries to the group, replied, "You said you created those new techniques for your students and that you were happy and proud of your achievement. It is good to feel that way sometimes because it is a part of growth. Nevertheless, you should bear in mind that creative work can only spring from two completely different sources: through the mind or through emptiness. The products of the mind and the products of emptiness are not the same; one is dealing with observable effects, the other involves one's inner being.

"If your work has sprung from the mind, that work is but a modification of something you have known with the mind. You did a little changing here and there of the old forms with which you are so familiar. You modified routines, altered movements to suit your personal taste. Understand that if the work is a modification of what you have known, nothing there can be called creative. Such would-be creation does not spring from the depths of your being. It is by nature superficial, and you must remain merely the skilled technician. Even so, you still have the right to be happy and proud of your achievement. Yes, it is gratifying to feel that way sometimes."

"Master, I do not understand."

The Master elaborated, "A technician works on an ordinary level and follows and imitates skillfully prearranged forms or traditional patterns. Any modification of such forms and patterns is simply a by-product of the intellect based on those patterns. One may be pleased with the modification, as you were, but that kind of satisfaction is ephemeral, a gust of wind that passes."

In deep thought, Master Tai-Anh moved to the open window, looked far off into the sky, shook his head, and slowly concluded, "What you need to discover is heavenly rapture, bliss. This is everlasting. Creativity through emptiness is blissful."

"Ah," said the student. There was a deep silence in the training hall. "Master, I still do not see the light."

"How can I explain light to you if you do not open your eyes? I have been illustrating and speaking of this matter for years, but still you remain deaf to my words and blind to my actions. You continue to accumulate new techniques even though you have not thoroughly assimilated the old ones. For more than twenty years you have worked at a superficial level, on the perimeter, the outer boundary, never yet entering the center.

"Once you are at the center, you are in a state of emptiness. The emptiness manifests itself only through a cleansing of your obstructing thoughts and feelings, a purification of false entities, a purging of material welfare, the illusions of the ordinary life. If you are to enter the realm of spirituality, you must attain a pure mind and an unstained heart. That purity is what this whole training of ours is about. One trains oneself to be a constructive, useful, and worthy human being—a human being human.

"When you refer to whatever you have acquired so far as creation, you trick yourself and merely feed your ego. No matter how lofty it may seem, the product of the outer mind is only a projection of your desire. Genuine creativity has no fixed patterns to follow, no criteria on which to rely, no paths to tread. It demands only a properly prepared consciousness to experience the unknown, and the truth miraculously enters your being. Then suddenly you perform techniques you have never performed before, you say something profound that you have never considered before. Your mind has dropped its shell and has allowed its inner mechanism to appear and take its course triumphantly. This prepared consciousness drives the fountain, and is the very source of all creative possibilities.

"You create something, but in that very act of creativity you utterly lose your identity, your self. You are no longer you. You become a mindless person; that is, a being free from mind. You become memoryless, but at that moment of becoming, memorylessness leads you to the unknown—to the truth. You do not aim to find the unknown. If you aim to find the unknown, the known appears instead, untruth comes forth. So remember, do not search for the truth. Do not search at all. This must be understood."

The Master then moved over to the window, remaining for many minutes lost in thought—and leaving the whole group in a quandary. One of the students complained to the others, "For many seminars the Master has repeated the same teachings, the same patterns, the same routines. We have been advised to remember things and train ourselves assiduously, and now he says that there are no patterns to follow, no criteria to rely upon, no paths to walk upon. Does he deceive us? Does he admit his whole teaching up to now is unreal, delusory?" The students pondered, dejected.

Let us attempt to discover what the Master means by speaking so equivocally. Perhaps he suggests something that is far beyond our ordinary comprehension, something that cannot be approached discursively. Or perhaps his expression implies something quite substantial, but beyond logic.

First, one should not forget that the Master typifies the attitude of the Asian master whose learned tendency is to speak what appears to be a language of nonsense, full of contradiction and ambiguity. In spite of the contradiction and ambiguity, Master Tai-Anh possesses the inmost nature of the authentic master. Without being conscious of his doing so, he creates odd situations that indirectly lead others to truth—or directly lead others to misjudge his attitude and misinterpret his words. He may appear occasionally senseless or inconsiderate; as a result, he may even become the target of covert ridicule and the object of doubts.

In fact, the Master had moved into a new plane of consciousness, a new dimension of training; but because the Master's change of direction occurred over time, his students were not able to perceive the difference.

Several times Master Tai-Anh had raised the mysterious veil of his changed state for his students, in order for them to have a new vision in their training, but they had persisted in the same illusions and had avoided being drawn into the deeper recesses of their consciousness. They were not able to get in touch with the ground of reality.

We must also understand that the authentic master never guides his students to originality, reality, or truth. It is impossible to do so. He can only guide them away from the path leading to unoriginality, unreality, and untruth. For originality cannot be taught, reality cannot be sought, and truth cannot be imparted to others. They are states for which one must prepare oneself, not by seeking but by living the purest life one is capable of living.

As teachers and masters are totally powerless to impart "truth," original techniques can emerge only through the devotion, faith, and unique experience of the student in spiritual life. By means of that unconsciously constant preparation, the development of self-realization is possible. In self-realization, anything one does is accomplished out of emptiness, beyond experiential differentiation, beyond subjectivity and objectivity, beyond time and space. Under such conditions, that which one does can be considered genuinely creative.

Emptiness can be achieved, but cannot be created. It is not a by-product of the intellect. If one intends to create it, then the intrusion of the senses is unavoidable. Created emptiness is not natural and free; it is not a key to the unknown, but is rather another barrier to the beyond. Regarding any phenomenon, originality can happen once and once only. A repetition becomes something second-hand, ready-made, not at all related to creativity.

Once a student asked Master Tai-Anh, "Do you remember now the counter-attack you demonstrated during the last class and, when we asked you to repeat it, said you had forgotten?" The Master smiled inwardly at his student's naive question and then, with a twinkle in his eyes replied, "Why do you wish me to remember? Do you believe that I should now retro-gress instead of progress?"

The student simply wanted the Master to repeat the technique that had so amazed the observers, but as the Master had lost his self during the performance, and had been functioning on a plane entirely different from that of consciousness, what then was available within him to remember? The inquiring student was not yet at a state enabling comprehension.

Nowadays there are copy machines in unlimited numbers and countless black-belt holders and teachers of every stripe and persuasion. In many occupations, the copy machine facilitates one's work; but in martial art, authentic teaching cannot tolerate the machine approach. The sincere student of martial art requires teachers who approach the art in a different state of being, a new state of being, a change of consciousness based in spirituality. This new state of being is necessary for authentic teaching. If it is necessary for the teacher, how can it not also be a sine qua non for the master, the mentor of teachers?

Those persons who become teachers without having

had the ethical grounding that is part and parcel of classical martial-arts training appear to misunderstand the purpose of their teaching. Many contemporary teachers languish in ignorance of the do's and don'ts that for centuries have been central to martial art. Thus the ethical component of each training phase for thousands upon thousands of students is very often absent. The void is filled with such things as considerations of game, entertainment, or sport—and material reward.

Of course teachers and students nowadays are free to follow whatever paths they choose, but in eschewing ethical training as the central issue, those teachers and students betray the mental or spiritual end which is the foremost aim of the authentic master. The teacher bears the far greater responsibility in this knowing or unknowing betrayal, for the student by definition arrives at the training hall in ignorance and trust.

Whereas it is true that game, entertainment, and sport can themselves be studied with high seriousness, scholarly seriousness must not be confused with spirituality. Teaching and learning martial-art routines as game, entertainment, and sport relegates art to the status of diversion.

Master Tai-Anh several times reminded his students to train themselves to become fully and creatively human in order to awaken their deeply hidden potential. He ended the training session by relating an anecdote to help clarify his lesson.

A customer wanted to buy a painting hung on the

wall of an art gallery, but the tag on the frame indicated, "Not for Sale." The customer was so taken with the painting that he sought out the artist and commissioned another work "just like the one that's not for sale."

A week later the customer returned to the gallery to pick up his order and saw what evidently was his painting leaning against the wall near the original. His copy was tagged "Sold." For a while he compared the two pieces of art with great satisfaction, observing the extraordinary likeness of the two works; but after a few moments, he felt inexplicably drawn to the original on the wall. He addressed the painter, "You know, there is something about the original there that I much prefer, even though I cannot describe what it is that attracts me, and I would very much appreciate it if you would sell me the original—now that you have a replacement."

"Sorry," said the painter, "I do not wish to do that. I am fond of it, too, and now you have a very satisfactory copy."

The customer said, "Look, these two paintings share the same setting, scenery, colors, composition, brush strokes. Even the canvas and the frames are the same appearance and quality. They look alike as two drops of water. What then is the difference? Why will you not grant my simple wish?"

The artist explained. "This painting that I am fond of is original. The painting you commissioned is an imitation. That is the difference."

The explanation did not much help the customer. He argued, "But the paintings are the product of the same artist. Both carry your signature!"

"Yes, both carry my signature, but when I worked on the copy I was an imitator. That signature is the signature of an imitator, not of a creator. When I gave birth to the original, it became unique; only one can exist in the whole world. If anyone wants to make a copy of it, he can produce as many copies as he wants. A reproduction is an imitation of the original, but it is not the original. Originality happens but once and no more."

At that moment a group of visitors entered the gallery, and the conversation ended. The customer went home with his copy, his mind not at ease. Some irresolvable matter still remained.

The story ended there, but Master Tai-Anh continued. "Can you guess who that customer was? Of course it was I."

"Master, you said you went home that day with something still bothering you. Does that something still bother you or have you found the solution?"

The Master welcomed the question. "That day I doubted the artist's interpretation and I regretted that time did not allow us to extend the discussion, but later I realized that the point the artist was arguing is akin to *The Way*.

"In martial art the traditional forms, the conventional routines, the basic techniques are designed to help the practitioner to get started, to get into the art.

But in further training, the student's clinging to technique becomes a barrier to progress.

"In painting, all the accouterments—canvas, easel, paint, brushes, and so forth—are necessary for the artist to enter into the art; but when the painting begins, the artist must ignore both materials and technique. The artist must paint without thinking about materials and technique. Only then is the painting original.

"Conventional technique must be discarded. Because of the very process of fabricating it, the imitation must lack spirituality. The hands and the head are not enough to create anything unique if the heart is missing, for that which we call heart is the attribute of the spirit, the essential element of the true artist."

Lam had been amazed throughout Master Tai-Anh's seminar. He felt the mysterious door to the martial arts had opened, but still he could not quite make his way through that opened door.

The mysterious, invisible power of ch'i had been
transmitted and received.

Chapter 14

AND YET ANOTHER LESSON

Budo is not a means of felling the opponent by force or by lethal weapons. Neither is it intended to lead the world to destruction by arms and other illegitimate means. True budo calls for bringing the inner energy of the universe in order, protecting the peace of the world and molding, as well as preserving, everything in nature in its right form. Training in budo is tantamount to strengthening, within my body and soul, the love of the deity who begets, preserves, and nurtures everything in nature.

—Morihei Ueshiba

IN THE DAYS following the seminar, Lam began to examine closely the mystery he felt, and most especially the words and actions of Master Tai-Anh. Lam saw nothing unusual or extraordinary about the Master's appearance or personality. The Master looked like everybody else, a simple human being, quiet and modest; but the way he talked, the way he acted, and the way he taught created a marvelously pleasing and trusting atmosphere. Lam felt confident with Master

Tai-Anh, confident and respectful, but all tinged with a little apprehension, a little anxiety.

Lam recalled having once met a Grand Master who spoke eloquently and who demonstrated many fabulous and ingenious techniques. Nevertheless, for some strange reason, these exhibitions by the Grand Master did not truly affect Lam's feelings and emotions. He did not feel drawn to the Grand Master as he did to Master Tai-Anh. So, one day Lam confided these inner feelings to Master Tai-Anh and asked the reason why it was so. What was the difference between the Grand Master's approach and that of Master Tai-Anh? And was there any secret to Tai-Anh's power?

Master Tai-Anh replied, "Nothing is secret, Lam. It is simply that the Grand Master had many things to talk about, many things to show to please people's eyes and answer people's expectations. As for me, I have nothing special to say or to show. This is the difference. Nothing is secret."

"There must be something different in you, then," Lam replied, "but I cannot figure it out. I would very much like to get to that mysterious something. Please teach me, enlighten me. This is my earnest desire!"

"Oh, not that!" laughed Master Tai-Anh. "Don't desire! You can get what you call that mysterious something for yourself, by yourself, but the very fact of your desiring it will work against your ever having it. Do not desire. It is one more attachment and it will lead you astray."

Lam remained quiet for a moment and then asked,

"But how can I give up desiring, because is not this wish-to-give-up-desiring a desire?"

The Master explained, "The problem is not in trying to give up anything, but in understanding what desire is and accepting it. Accept it calmly because it is already there. You cannot avoid it. It cannot go away. It cannot disappear unless you accept it totally, completely."

"Please clarify for me how to accept it and accept it totally, calmly," Lam pressed on.

"Simply accept it without question; allow desire simply to happen. Consider it as a part of your being. Watch it, note it, be with it, even enjoy it. Otherwise you will create an antagonism, an ever-present conflict in yourself between giving it up or not giving it up, desiring or not desiring. If your desire should not be fulfilled, you will always desire that happy ending wherein the desire comes to fruition. And even if a desire were to come to a happy conclusion, another desire will surely take its place, then another will follow, and then another, and so on into the whirlpool of confusion. If there is any secret to all this, the secret is to bring forth a new consciousness; that is, the absence of desire."

Observing Lam's puzzled expression, Master Tai-Anh clarified his statement further. "What I mean by absence of desire is this: If you are able to see desired things without personal attachment arising in your mind, then your mind is free from desiring and attaching. On the other hand, if you experience things that you do not desire, that you find distinctly undesirable, and you view them with repulsion, then your mind is once again imprisoned. When these two forms are absent, you mind is unstained, clear, void, empty, and totally in the flow of the *Tao*. This is what I mean by absence of desire."

Although Master Tai-Anh's words were clear, Lam was not able to fathom their meaning. His mind turned to another curiosity. He said, "Master, there is a problem that has bothered me for some time. I seem to lose my understanding of *ch'i* even after long hours of practice and meditation. The essence of it still eludes me. In fact, sometimes I wonder if I have the ability to know the source of it."

Master Tai-Anh smiled and responded in a leisurely tone. "Come, Lam. Serve me a cup of tea, and we can talk it over." Sipping his tea from time to time, Master Tai-Anh began to speak. "So, let us begin our attempt to understand this mysterious energy called *ch'i*. *Ch'i* is a term that involves great complexity of understanding, cultivation, and development. *Ch'i* refers to the vivifying principle in Chinese cosmology. It means breath, vapor, air, steam, vital fluid, force, temper, feelings, human energy, and the psychophysical power associated with blood and breath. It means all of these things. Yes, *ch'i* is a complex concept indeed!

"It is complex, and yet its complexity depends on the context in which we view it. Have you not learned, Lam, that in every field of endeavor, we should have a right view of that endeavor? By right view I mean a faith, a loyalty, a sincere devotion to what we are doing."

"Indeed, Master, I would say that a right view is what you have been expecting me to cultivate these many years," responded Lam, who was now listening very carefully.

"Precisely," said Master Tai-Anh. "And as our rightness of view increases, our understanding of *ch'i* becomes clearer. It becomes very simple.

"In our field of martial art, *ch'i* refers to vital energy, to motive force, to intrinsic bio-energy. In Eastern thought, especially in traditional Eastern medicine, this vital energy exists within the human body before the body is even brought to life." The Master paused to sweep some bread crumbs from the cutting board into his hand. He opened the nearby window and gently threw the crumbs to some magpies which had gathered near the window. "According to this belief," he continued, "there are two kinds of *ch'i* that lie within the body: the prenatal *ch'i* that is the motive force, and the postnatal *ch'i*, the material force."

"What is the difference between the two?" Lam inquired.

"Prenatal *ch'i*, sometimes called congenital or primary *ch'i*, is inherited from our parents during our formation into the fetus. The postnatal *ch'i* comes later, referring to the air we breathe, the food we eat, and the nurture we receive following our birth. Each works separately to produce energy for use by our body-mind-spirit. But whenever they are in imbalance with each other, lopsided in relationship to one another, we become diseased in some way. In martial art, it is of primary importance to keep these energies in balance so as to promote health. When we are in excellent health, *ch'i* circulates freely through specific channels."

Master Tai-Anh breathed deeply, sipped some more tea and continued. "Over centuries, the idea of cultivating and balancing *ch'i* to circulate within the body to ensure good health occupied Eastern thinking as a primary consideration. However, cultivating and developing *ch'i* is not only to preserve health and prolong life, but also to be able to treat and cure illnesses and diseases. In this regard, most authentic martial-art masters of the past were also skilled healers. Like physicians, they had professional obligations to humanity. They were persons of conscience who understood keenly and personally the nature of sacrifice for the sake of the art.

"Nowadays, unfortunately, such masters have become exceedingly rare, perhaps almost an extinct species. The great majority of practitioners are so completely seduced by the blandishments of wealth, fame, power, and prestige that finally they lose that with which they surely began their teaching: they lose their passion to fulfill their sacred duty."

Master Tai-Anh sat silent, pensive, for a few moments, and then proceeded. "And because of this, Lam, because of this, more and more genuine martial-arts masters are losing understanding of their mission and their proper status." Master Tai-Anh paused again.

"My fondest dream is that you, Lam, and others of your generation will revitalize martial art so that it can regain its integrity and become once again part of the healing arts!"

"May I ask," said Lam, "what kinds of illnesses and diseases a true master can actually heal?"

"Various kinds of pain and suffering are relieved by *ch'i-kung* techniques. Starting with bruises, muscle pain, broken bones, sprains, and so on. Later, the most skilled masters may treat arthritis, hypertension, heart disease, diabetes, peptic ulcer, and—today—certain types of cancer."

"That's amazing! But why have none of my other teachers taught this to me, Master? Is it kept a secret?"

"No, it is not a secret at all. It is simply that, although many martial-arts masters have heard about these healing methods, many have never had the opportunity to be trained and, because of this, have not the ability to train others in the healing arts. You must understand that *ch'i* and *ch'i-kung* cannot be understood without practical experience. Mere words are not enough. Technical transmission through the reading of books gives only a superficial knowledge which tends to mislead and cloud its reality. Nowadays the martial-arts teachers so busy teaching fancy tricks of fighting meant to impress others, are not taking up the challenge and making the time to learn these hidden methods of holistic healing."

Lam tried to calm his sudden desire to learn some secrets and said softly, "What are the hidden parts of the training that you are talking about, Master? What are the requirements that might enable me to learn them?"

"When it is time you will be ready to learn, and I will be there to teach you. But for now your monkey mind is still jumping here and there enjoying insignificant and superficial things. When it is time, we shall work on *ch'i-kung* and other things. As of now your mind is not yet calm. You wish to know the requirements. There is nothing special, but a total relaxation, a quietness of mind and body before attempting to begin. And this type of relaxation involves certain methods of breathing, contains static and dynamic exercises to allow the manipulative psychokinetics to begin to function. This *ch'i* enables a tremendous influence of mind over matter without the intermediation of physical force. In this respect, *ch'i-kung* exercises are more advanced."

"What does *ch'i-kung* mean, Master? I have heard you use this term a number of times, but I have not quite got the meaning."

"*Ch'i-kung* means the ability or skill of breathing to bring about psychophysiological power. Its activities have been very much influenced by Chinese internal systems of kung-fu, the arts which the Chinese refer to collectively as *wu-shu*, including t'ai-chi ch'uan, *pa-kua chang*, and *hsing-i ch'uan*. So you can understand that *ch'i-kung* is a branch of kung-fu in which we work toward acquiring inner strength by means of breathing and exercising to keep the mind and body in good and balanced condition. We do this, of course, in order to be able to face emergencies as well as to be able to call on *ch'i* for preventing and curing various illnesses and diseases."

Lam mused, "In that case, *ch'i-kung* belongs to the medical field, and it is because it is very difficult to learn you do not wish to teach me. Is this true, Master?"

"It is true that *ch'i-kung* has always been tied to Asian medical science. Although the actual practice of *ch'i-kung* looks simple and effortless, the training to perform it entails long and laborious work. The essence of the training is learning how to arouse the dormant *ch'i* and use it for therapeutic purposes.

"Now, the reason I have not taught you is that this type of training requires the patience and the faith to perform prescribed monotonous exercises daily, and I have found you to have but a very small reserve of those characteristics, Lam. You want to learn everything now. You want to accumulate new things each day and as a result of this desire, you grasp nothing at the end. Nothing."

This analysis of Lam's learning style was so right that it touched the student's heart. Trying to hide his embarrassment, he asked calmly, "How long does it take to arouse the dormant *ch'i*, Master?"

"Normally, Lam, for one who is able to exercise the discipline necessary to perform the exercises, it takes a minimum of one hundred days of training to fulfill the bare essentials. It takes one thousand days of highly focused work to get *ch'i* to circulate within the body."

"Ah. That long, Master!" exclaimed Lam in surprise.

"Not only that, but the requirements are not simply limited to a daily ration of exercises, but depend also on other factors such as proper diet and an appropriate style of living, of work, sleep, of social habits, and so forth. For these reasons few in our time can master the art. Those who have mastered it have the ability to do incredible things. They can directly influence physical objects; that is, they can exercise mind over matter. Yes, they can move objects without touching them physically. They can, for example, use their external *ch'i* to light a fluorescent tube. Fantastic? Fact! They can emit their *ch'i* to various areas of a patient's body during surgical operations, obviating the use of conventional anesthesia."

Lam closed his gaping jaw and then said, "It all sounds like, like science fiction, like mythology, like fakery."

Master Tai-Anh's demeanor was grave. He nodded in agreement. "Yes, it does, but it is physically verifiable reality. The emission of *ch'i* involves various forms of what Western science refers to as infrared radiation, static electricity, and wave-interference patterns. Scientists who experience *ch'i* emitted by competent Eastern practitioners are mind-boggled, for the powerful phenomena they feel are inconsistent with the theories they have learned. They usually depart from such experiences shaken to their roots."

Master Tai-Anh paused, looked intently at Lam, and smiled. Slowly and with great deliberation, Master

Tai-Anh extended his external *ch'i* through his right palm, the fingers directed toward Lam, sitting three feet away. Lam felt a powerful jolt and a heavy pressure against his chest which caused him to fall back into his chair, his eyes open wide in astonishment. Lam closed his eyes, breathed deeply, and absorbed the invisible power which now seemed to flood the training hall.

Lam pondered the demonstration in silence. Master Tai-Anh rose up and left the hall. The message had been transmitted and received. Tai-Anh smiled again and nodded to himself: Lam would learn. He would perhaps learn slowly, but he would learn.

This sword will not be an ordinary weapon destined
to kill any sentient being. It will kill only my own
greed, arrogance, anger, and folly.

Chapter 15

A Master is Born

Which tree is blooming
I cannot from here discern,
But its fragrance—ah!

—Basho

YEARS PASSED. Lam excelled in the eyes of his teachers, left Master Tai-Anh's school, and became very successful as a martial-arts teacher. So many students rushed to his classes that he opened other schools. In the opinion of the world, Lam was enormously successful. But on that fateful day when Lam had visited Master Tai-Anh accompanied by a demanding customer and had been rebuffed by the Master, Lam realized that he was still not whole, still not yet in touch with his human potential. And so a soul-shaken Lam made the decision to return once again to his Master's school for further training. Master Tai-Anh had retired from teaching into contemplation at his cottage on an island some distance away.

One morning after Lam had assumed the role of student once more, in the midst of Lam's regular hour devoted to contemplation, another of the many discussions between teachers took place. This one involved two teachers arguing about the ups and downs of present-day martial arts, its splendid fighting skills as contrasted with its decadence of moral fiber among both leaders and practitioners. Other teachers, one by one, joined in the discussion, which quickly became an argument. As was the habit of these teachers, they would gossip about each other, repeat rumors, project plans to bring in more business, and devise various ways to advertise themselves and improve their positions. Lam found such discussions unpleasant, unproductive, destructive; but he recalled Master Tai-Anh's observation that deeds, not words, define the person.

Lam sought only quiet and serenity for his contemplation. Though immersed daily in this very materialistic and competitive atmosphere, Lam was now able to transcend the distractions and reside on a totally different plane. The teachers were much aware of Lam's history, his struggles against egotism and the blandishments of the world, and his evidently special relationship with Master Tai-Anh. The teachers could not help but witness the depth and consistency of Lam's mindfulness. One by one, they came to admire and marvel at Lam's attitude, his integrity, his martial-arts excellence, as well as the power to heal, an art on which he had concentrated much of his energy in recent years. The teachers agreed among themselves that of all the residents of the school—men and women, students and teachers alike—Lam was the person of whom they were most respectful. They agreed to present Lam with the rare, honorific title of Master and to make the presentation ceremoniously.

The ceremony and reception for Lam had been joyful and a festive atmosphere pervaded the training hall. But when Lam was called to make the formal acknowledgment of his new honor before the assembled students, teachers, and dignitaries from the city, something most unexpected unfolded.

As the applause ceased after the award, all eyes were directed at the new Master. But Lam remained for many minutes in a kneeling position, silent and motionless, facing the expectant audience. Then, saying nothing, Lam rose and began moving, raising his arms gently and slowly, up and down, down and up, advancing and retreating, left and right, right and left in sometimes rapid circular motions and in sometimes slow spirals. Lam performed with the graceful movements similar to those he had secretly witnessed Master Tai-Anh perform, years before, outside the Master's cottage.

The performance at times resembled a soft t'ai-chi ch'uan routine, sometimes like aikido with its circular motions, and sometimes hopping and wriggling like *t'ai-mantis* kung-fu. The presentation did not conform with any conventional or traditional patterns, was not a recognizable routine. Empty of all constraint, the performance, beautiful as any they had ever seen, nevertheless shocked the audience.

Why was it that Lam said nothing? Why did he not remark about his training experiences or cite his many achievements as so many honorees had done before him? Why did he not offer words of thanks to his teacher, Master Tai-Anh, and to his other teachers, and bid a fond farewell to his fellow students? What was to be gained by his remaining silent and displaying only extraordinary movements throughout the ceremony?

The unfamiliar movements in empty space answered all these questions, and themselves comprised Lam's message. His silence sang so beautifully and his emptiness filled the space about him so wonderfully that his audience was unable to comprehend it. The movements Lam performed were not Lam's at all, at least not the part of Lam that arose from his ego and his persona. In this sense, it was not Lam performing. The performance was able to happen because Lam was emanating from his deepest, innermost core of being. No ego-centered motivation or maneuvering was present in his gentle and delicate movements. The movements were possible because Lam was both out of his mind in the most profound sense of that expression and into the here-and-now of his existence. The performance became a performance without a performer, so exceptional, so unconventional and untraditional that the audience found it difficult to conceive and absorb its message.

Lam left the school then, stopping at the gate only momentarily to reminisce, to admire the old buildings sparkling in the morning sun, and to recall that long-gone day when, as an arrogant young district chief he had been humbled by a righteous Master Tai-Anh. Lam decided to first visit his family and then to try once again to meet Master Tai-Anh, whom he had not seen since that humiliating trip to Tai-Anh's cottage years before. He remembered how that visit, with the door slammed in his face, had shaken free Lam's long-neglected need for endless self-questioning about his direction and motivation, about his work as a martial-arts teacher—and about his greed, his arrogance, and his persistent ignorance. He would try to show Master Tai-Anh that perhaps it was now time.

One afternoon some days later, Lam paddled a little boat, weighed down with all his belongings, to the island of Master Tai-Anh. As Lam approached the shore, he felt a chill in the air and noted an unusual darkness instead of the glaring afternoon sun of a few minutes before. As he docked he saw a man he identified as the new National President and a number of women and men whom he recognized as Master Tai-Anh's former students. All stood facing the Master's cottage, their heads bowed in sadness.

Lam's old friendly adversary, Hau, approached first and informed him quietly that Master Tai-Anh was on the brink of death. Lam's breath caught in his chest upon hearing the news. Tears welled in his eyes and his shoulders sagged.

As Hau escorted Lam into the cottage, Lam stopped at the entrance to Master Tai-Anh's room and looked up over the doorway at the beautiful sword hanging there. Even though it was filmed with dust and strung with cobwebs, he recognized it as Master Tai-Anh's favorite, the very sword Lam had longed for as a young student. Attached to the sword was a card lettered in

Master Tai-Anh's delicate hand: "For the One Who Has Moral Strength."

Entering Master Tai-Anh's room, Lam felt gloom and loss. He approached the bed and realized then that the Master was barely breathing. A deep sadness mixed with affection wove in and out of Lam's entire being. Bending over the Master's bed, Lam touched the old man's hand and whispered, "Master, this is Lam, your incorrigible student. I have returned to be by your side. Do you hear me?" Master Tai-Anh made no response and his emaciated body made no movement. Lam's heart sank but he resolved to try his best to help his Master.

Lam closed his eyes, breathed deeply, and called on his body to arouse *ch'i* to proportions he had never before attempted. In the great stillness which enveloped his being, Lam inhaled deeply once again and lowered his hands, emitting the external *ch'i* to certain parts of Master Tai-Anh's all but lifeless body. He held each point on the body for many minutes, summoning all the healing energy from the center of his being, through his hands, and into the body of his beloved Master. But nothing happened. There was not the slightest response. Beads of perspiration gathered on his forehead and streams of exhalation hissed through his throat as Lam tried again and again, but Master Tai-Anh remained motionless. Perplexed and distressed beyond measure, Lam bowed and withdrew quietly from the room. All that his Master had taught him of the art of healing, all that he had learned in subsequent years, had been for naught. Lam sobbed as he left the cottage.

Returning to the boat to gather his belongings, Lam stopped along the path to pick a lone white lotus flower from the edge of the lake. Staring at the complex geometry of its closing petals, Lam was brought back to his meditations in that small corner of the training hall in the Master's school, and countless memories flooded his mind: of his overbearing conduct with Master Tai-Anh during his very first boat trip to the capital; then of his becoming attendant to the National Teacher and then Chief of District, a troublemaker out to replace the Master's school with his own puerile project; and then to his life as a famous martial-arts teacher, a money-maker; and, finally, as a healer. The memories faded and affection and gratitude for his Master overcame him. Tears of love and grief streamed down his cheeks.

His decision was made, the choice was clear that he would care for his teacher until the final moment of life. Then he would retreat somewhere, anywhere, away from the tumult of the world, perhaps on an island far away.

As Lam sat in the boat, recovering the energy expended during his attempt to heal Master Tai-Anh, the boat drifted lazily from the dock. Suddenly the stillness was broken by a strange sound coming across the water. Lam's eyes shot open and he beheld heading directly toward him, Master Tai-Anh running on the surface of the shimmering lake, his slipper-shod feet flying over the water making that odd sound, a sword swinging from his waving arm, joy radiating through his sparkling eyes. Lam's heart fluttered and he crouched transfixed in the boat as the Master reached his side.

The Master gently placed his hand on Lam's shoulder and said, "Lam! The time is not right for you to dwell in seclusion, to isolate yourself from the world." Gazing deeply into Lam's astonished eyes, Master Tai-Anh continued. "Instead, it is time for you to share your insights with others in the correct path of training. Bring love, compassion, and justice to your fellow beings. As a martial-arts adept, you must contribute your part to society. That is where you belong. Do not be selfish and consider only yourself. You have not yet reached your ultimate destiny." So saying, the Master extended the sword to Lam.

Almost stupefied by Master Tai-Anh's appearance and his incredible feat, as well as by his telepathic powers, Lam could only look with mouth agape into Master Tai-Anh's radiant face. Master and student appeared to be locked in that starry gaze, exchanging silent thoughts, waiting for something from each other.

In a solemn voice Lam said, "Dear Master, I pledge to you that I will pursue your will to return to society with this sacred sword." Reaching for the sword with both hands, Lam saw that the lotus was still clutched between his fingers, its petals now open and radiant in the twilight. He handed the flower gently to his

Master. Lam took the sword and solemnly raised it to his forehead with both hands, making a vow: "This sword, I assure you, will not be an ordinary weapon destined to kill any sentient being. It will kill only my own greed, arrogance, anger, and folly. It will not be an object of destruction, but a symbol of constructive deeds, of justice, of compassion, and love. I vow to take responsibility to perform only the purest of deeds and to live in service to all living, feeling beings. I promise never to dishonor your teachings."

Glancing down at the blossom nestled in his wrinkled hands and then back at Lam, Master Tai-Anh's peaceful face was filled with happiness. "Master Lam!" he said. The smile on his lips turned to a broad grin, and then to gales of the deepest laughter, laughter which broke the stillness of the twilight. Master Lam's own smile also exploded into joyful, uncontrollable laughter until, in unison, their laughter became one sound which echoed across water and mountain into the welcome of the serene evening, filling the universe with their love and compassion for each other in the *Tao*.

Epigraph References

Blyth, R. H. *Chinese Ancient Fables*. Beijing: Foreign Languages Press, 1981.

Miyamoto, Musashi. *A Book of Five Rings: The Classic Guide to Strategy*. Woodstock, New York: The Overlook Press, 1974.

Ueshiba, Kisshomaru. *The Spirit of Aikido*. Tokyo: Kodansha International, 1984.